THE PREEMINENCE OF CHRIST

PART ONE

I0191303

TO THE
GLORY
OF GOD THE FATHER

SPENCER STEWART

PROJECT ONE 28

LAWRENCE, KANSAS

The Preeminence of Christ:
Part One, To the Glory of God the Father

Second Edition, Copyright © 2017 by Spencer Stewart

Published by Project one28
      P. O. Box 442135
      Lawrence, KS 66044

www.ProjectOne28.com

Cover Image: Denis Belitsky (Shutterstock)
Cover Design: Tyler Norris
           www.tylernorris.me

First Printing 2017
Printed in the United States of America

Paperback ISBN: 978-0-9961867-2-8
Epub ISBN: 978-0-9961867-4-2
Mobipocket ISBN: 978-0-9961867-5-9

Scripture quotations, unless otherwise noted, are from *The Holy Bible, English Standard Version*, copyright © 2001 by Crossway Bibles, a division of Good News Publishers, though always amending the mistranslation "the LORD" or "GOD" (in SMALL CAPS) to Yahweh or Yah.

Italics in Biblical quotations indicate emphasis added by the author.

PUBLISHER'S CATALOGING-IN-PUBLICATION DATA

Names: Stewart, Spencer Blake, author.
Title: The preeminence of Christ : part one , to the glory of God the father / Spencer Stewart.
Identifiers: ISBN 978-0-9961867-2-8 | LCCN 2016949810
Series: The Preeminence of Christ
Description: Includes index and bibliographical references. | Second edition. | Lawrence, KS: Project one28, 2017.
Subjects: LCSH Jesus Christ. | Christianity. | Bible. New Testament -- Criticism, interpretation, etc. | Son of God. | Divine man (Christology). | BISAC RELIGION / Christian Theology / Christology
Classification: LCC BT205.S857 2017 | DDC 232.8 -- dc23

Thanks, God, for directing the steps of Nathan Hiebert, who let Your light shine into my blindness so that I saw Your worth and glorified You as the Father of our Lord Jesus Christ, and for bringing Chris Waipa at the right time to set my life and ministry on the trajectory to write – ten years later – a book such as this for Your glory.

PSALM 115:1 (AT)
Not to us, Yahweh, not to us
But to Your Name give glory
Because of Your loyal love
Because of Your faithfulness

CONTENTS

CONTENTS (CONTINUED)

ABBREVIATIONS

AT	Author's Translation
BDAG	*A Greek-English Lexicon of the New Testament and Other Early Christian Literature,* Third Edition
cf.	*confer,* compare
e.g.	*exempli gratia,* for example
ESV	*The Holy Bible, English Standard Version*
Gk.	Greek (language)
HCSB	*Holman Christian Standard Bible*
Hb.	Hebrew (language)
i.e.	*id est,* that is (in other words)
lit.	literally
LITV	*Literal Translation of the Holy Bible,* Jay P. Green
LXX	Septuagint (Greek Old Testament)
n.	footnote (or, heaven forbid: endnote)
NASB	*The New American Standard Bible*
NBD	*New Bible Dictionary,* Third Edition
NET	*The New English Translation*
NIDNTT	*New International Dictionary of New Testament Theology*
NIV	*Holy Bible, New International Version*
NKJV	*The New King James Version*
NT	New Testament
OT	Old Testament
p. (pp.)	page (pages)
Pace	Latin: "in peace," employed to express polite disagreement
TWOT	*Theological Wordbook of the Old Testament*
v. (vv.)	verse (verses)

AGREEING WITH GOD'S PLAN

This is an evil age (Gal. 1:4), but God's plan to fix it is perfect. His plan should be our plan. His goal should be our goal. Three passages of Scripture in particular articulate God's administration of His world to accomplish His goal for it, and these passages set the trajectory for this series:

> COLOSSIANS 1:15-20 (AT)
> [The Son] [15]who is the image of the unseen God,
> the firstborn over all creation,
> [16]because by Him all things were created
> in the heavens and on the earth –
> the visible things and the invisible things,
> whether thrones or dominions
> or rulers or authorities –
> all things have been created through Him and for Him;
> [17]and He Himself is before all things,
> and in Him all things have stayed together,
> [18]and He Himself is the Head of the Body, the Assembly;
> who is the beginning,
> the firstborn from the dead,

in order that He Himself may have preeminence in all things,,
[19]because in Him all the fullness was pleased to dwell,
[20]and through Him to reconcile all things to Himself,
having made peace through the blood of His Cross,
through Him, whether the things, on the earth
or the things, in the heavens.

EPHESIANS 1:9-10 (AT)
…having made known to us the mystery of, His will,
according to His good pleasure, which He set forth in Him
[Christ], for *an, economy*[1] *of, the fullness of, the times, to head
up*[2] *all things in Christ*, things in the heavens and things in the
earth – in Him.

PHILIPPIANS 2:9-11 (AT)
[8]He humbled Himself,
having become obedient unto death,
        even death by a, cross.
[9]And therefore God highly exalted Him
and gave to, Him the Name
        that is, above every name,
[10]in order that at the Name of, Jesus
every knee may bow,
        heavenly and earthly and under-worldly,
[11]and every tongue confess that
Jesus Christ is, Lord –
        unto the, glory of, God the, Father!

God plans to glorify Himself by saving and transforming
disciples into the image of His crucified and resurrected Son,
Jesus Christ, who will return soon to overcome every enemy and

---

1. *Oikonomia*, from which we derive "economy," is house law (*oikos* plus *nomos*),
    administration or management to accomplish a purpose, a plan (cf. *BDAG*, 697;
    Jürgen Goetzmann, "House," *NIDNTT*, 2:255).

2. A combination of NIV (1984) and NASB ("to sum up under one head") may best
    translate the tricky Greek verb, since *anakephalaioō* can mean to bring together
    and to sum up under a ledger entry (Rom. 13:9, *BDAG*, 65), and it is built
    upon the word *kephalē*, "head." Colin Brown says this verb "means to bring
    something to a *kephalaion* [head], to sum up, recapitulate" ("Head," *NIDNTT*,
    2:163). *Pace* Peter T. O'Brien (*The Letter to the Ephesians*, PNTC (Grand Rapids,
    MI: Eerdmans, 1999], 111, n. 97), I believe the contextual proximity and

to saturate everything with His glory in a new, heavenly earth, in which God will tabernacle forever.[3] Ephesians 1:9-10 describes this plan as summing up all things under Christ's headship, that is, His benevolent rule. Colossians 1:18 encapsulates it as Christ's preeminence, His having the first and supreme place with respect to all things. When Christ is preeminent in every heart and action on earth and in the heavens, then God's glory will be unhindered and His purposes fully realized.

God never fails. His plan is so certain that it can be spoken of in the past tense as having already been accomplished (e.g., Eph. 3:11, Rom. 8:30). His plan is so invincible that visions of the future can been seen in the present (e.g., Rev. 21-22). God will indeed fill a new, heavenly earth with His glory through the preeminence of His Son, Jesus Christ. *What a glorious Being this Jesus must be since He is able to accomplish[4] the eternal purposes of God!*

If we are to agree with God's plan and participate in His success, then we must continually be learning to allow Christ to be preeminent in all things in our lives: the thoughts and intentions of our hearts, our relationships, our time, money, and ambitions. We must be learning to interpret all things (the Scriptures, our circumstances, the whole of reality in heaven and earth) through the lens of Christ's preeminence.[5] By beholding the glory of Christ and, therefore, submitting to His Lordship,

---

thematic centrality of "head" in Eph. 1:22 (also 4:15, 5:23, cf. "body" in 1:23, 2:16, 3:6; 4:4, 12, 16; 5:23, 30) warrants a translation of 1:10 that contains "head." Cf. the translation and study note by NET, "to head up."

3. With Eph. 1:9-10; Col. 1:15-20; Phil. 2:9-11, see Rom. 8:29-30; 2 Cor. 3:18; Eph. 1:23; 1 Cor. 15:24-28; Rev. 21:1-3, 11, 22-23; 22:5; Num. 14:21, Rom. 11:36.

4. Eph. 3:11 says God has already "accomplished" His eternal purpose in Christ. What remains to be done is not categorically new risk, but the inevitable outworking of Christ's victory in His death and resurrection.

5. I still remember this "lens" teaching from Sam McVay, Jr., "The Supremacy of Christ," 12 Sept 2004 (NewLifeEquip.com/resourcelibrary.cfm?id=8592). In it (as in most of his sermons of that era) he also made fun of my long rock star hair (as he should have).

we are being transformed by His Spirit into His image from glory to glory (2 Cor. 3:18). That is my motivation and excitement for this series. I long to boast about Christ and to teach the riches of Scripture's revelation of His glory so that we will be transformed by beholding it, and He will be praised as He deserves. I earnestly pray for this series to fortify our allegiance to Christ and our joyful submission to the increase of His government and peace.[6]

Part One will labor to make clear from the start what is the point of all this: God's glory. God's glory is the highest goal, and it is more than an abstract concept. Glory is a Person: God the Son. Therefore, the succeeding parts of this series will focus in depth on the titles Scripture gives to this glorious Jesus, such as the I AM, Lord, God, the Word, the Son of God and the Son of Man, the Christ, the Son of David, the Servant, the Lamb of God, the Last Adam and Second Man, the Firstborn, the Head of His Body, King of kings, and Heir of all things! What do these titles mean? How should they affect us? He alone is truly worthy of these names and worthy that we would "marvel" at Him because of them.[7]

---

6. Isa. 9:6-7
7. Jn. 5:20; cf. Mt. 8:27, 15:31; 2 Thess. 1:10

MOST VALUABLE

To value most some lesser thing is sinful. For example, if I consider myself the most important thing in my life, then I am sinning because I am not truly most valuable. God is perfect so, by nature, God values most that which is most valuable.[1] What is most valuable? God! God is the most valuable Being in existence, so God values Himself above all else. To put it another way, the most important thing to God is God.

Even seasoned, brilliant Biblical scholars can stumble at the declaration that the most important thing to God is Himself.[2] It may sound so egotistical and self-absorbed. We recoil when humans are narcissistic. How could God be like that? Let us know clearly: the holy God is not like sinful Man. He is uncreated; He does not owe His existence to anyone or anything. He is

---

1. See John Piper, *Desiring God: Meditations of a Christian Hedonist* (Sisters, OR: Multnomah, 2003), 42-43.

2. It seems to me that God's ultimate passion for His own glory ruffles those who think it diminishes His "selfless" love for us. However, love itself should be defined in the context of glory, as is done on pp. 73-77 (esp. n. 10). A couple of scholars with this struggle have been deftly answered by Dr. James M. Hamilton, Jr., in *God's Glory in Salvation*

not lesser than anything; He is infinitely the greatest. He is not sinful like us; He is perfect. Therefore, the descriptions given to sinners, such as selfish, do not apply to God. He is in a category of His own. God's valuing Himself above all else is not sinful, like prizing self would be for us. For God, it is right and true and holy because He *is* in reality the greatest worth!

On the other hand, if God would ever value something else more than Himself, *then* He would be sinning. *To sin* literally means "to miss the mark." Therefore, in a teaching session, I once found myself drawing the following illustration:

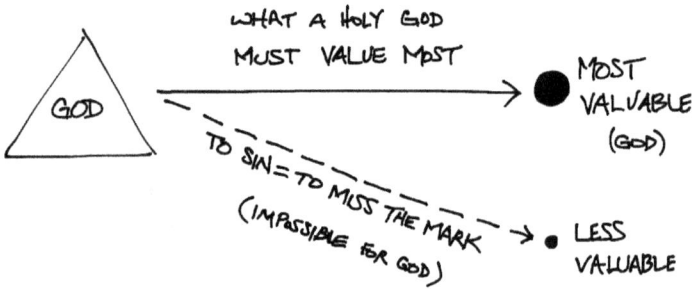

GLORY

God's greatest goal in all of His works is Himself – His glory, His Name. We will look at Scriptures that clearly substantiate this, but first let us be sure we understand the terms. *Glory* is one of those words that is used so frequently in the Scriptures that we can begin to take it for granted without being conscious of its full meaning or significance. *Glory is the manifestation of one's nature that results in praise and fame.*[3] Sometimes glory refers directly to the praise that is the result of seeing the manifestation

---

through Judgment: A Biblical Theology (Wheaton, IL: Crossway, 2010), 560-562. See also John Piper, "Why Oprah and Brad Pitt Deserted God (And Why You Shouldn't)" (vimeo.com/51407893).

3. For supporting quotations, see ProjectOne28.com/GloryDefinition. In *Theology 101 for Kids!* I define glory as "the shining of who God is" (ProjectOne28.com/kids).

of one's being (e.g., "Give God the glory [honor and praise] due to Him").[4]

God's glory is the *radiance* of His Being, which brings Him praise. Among John Piper's many helpful words on the glory of God, I particularly like his simple definition: "the *going public* of his infinite worth."[5] He also writes of it as "the beauty and greatness of God's manifold perfections" because "specific aspects of God's being are said to have glory. For example: 'the glory of his grace' (Ephesians 1:6) and 'the glory of his might' (2 Thessalonians 1:9)."[6] God's glory is the *shining forth* of His holiness,[7] goodness, power, love, justice, mercy, etc. When God *shows* Himself, He glorifies Himself.

God's ultimate reason for everything He does is to glorify Himself. As we will see below, even though the salvation of Man is popularly thought to be the greatest goal and theme in the Bible, it is actually subordinate. Redemption is a means to the ultimate end: God's glory. We need to align our hearts with God's ultimate goal so that we can put all subordinate means in perspective. It is my prayer that such will be a fruit of this book.

---

4. E.g., 1 Chron. 16:28-29; Isa. 42:8, Jer. 13:15. Tremper Longman III writes, "Fourth, glory elicits praise. Indeed, the verb related to the noun *kabod* may be translated 'praised.' In other words, to 'glorify' someone is to attribute weight or substance to him" ("The Glory of God in the Old Testament" in *The Glory of God,* ed. Christopher W. Morgan & Robert A. Peterson [Wheaton, IL: Crossway, 2010], 78). Richard R. Melick, Jr., adds, "In Matthew and Mark the noun *glory* involves a revelation of true character, while the verb involves acknowledging that character. People 'glorify' by appreciating the character observed" ("The Glory of God in the Synoptic Gospels, Acts, and the General Epistles," in *ibid.,* 82).

5. John Piper, "What is God's glory?" 6 Jul 2009 (desiringGod.org/interviews/what-is-gods-glory, emphasis mine).

6. John Piper, "Rebuilding Some Basics of Bethlehem: The Centrality of the Glory of God," 4 Nov 2009 (desiringGod.org/articles/rebuilding-some-basics-of-bethlehem-the-centrality-of-the-glory-of-god).

7. Piper teaches the unique connection of holiness and glory through Isaiah 6:3. The seraphim in the temple were crying, "Holy, holy, holy is Yahweh of hosts; the whole earth is full of his..." – where Piper inserts his point: "you would expect them to say 'holiness' and they say 'glory'" (n. 3). Therefore, he teaches, "The holiness of God is his concealed glory. The glory of God is his revealed holiness" ("To Him Be Glory

God does everything for His own sake, and again, this is right and good – and, as we will see, good for us.[8] That God does everything for His sake does not mean that He does not act for our sake, because *we* exist for His sake. When He acts for us, He is acting for Himself because we are purposed for Him. Consider both in the petition of Psalm 109:21: "deal on *my behalf* for *your name's sake*" (cf. Isa. 30:18). The truth will de-center us, but it will also draw us properly into God's central and ultimate aim, in which His redeemed, adopted children share His joy in the glory of His One-of-a-kind Son. As Jonathan Edwards wrote:

> God in seeking his glory seeks the good of his creatures, because the emanation of his glory... implies the... happiness of his creatures. And in communicating his fullness for them, he does it for himself, because their good, which he seeks, is so much in union and communion with himself. God is their good.... God, in seeking their glory and happiness, seeks himself, and in seeking himself, *i.e.* himself diffused... he seeks their glory and happiness. [9]

Therefore, God is *loving us* when He relates to us *for Himself.*

NAME

As we study the abundance of scriptures asserting God's glory as the greatest goal, we will notice that many verses focus on the

---

Forevermore," 17 Dec 2006 (desiringGod.org/messages/to-him-be-glory-forevermore). Piper also points to the parallelism in Leviticus 10:3: "'I will be shown to be *holy* among those who are near me, and before all the people I will be *glorified*.' When God shows himself to *be* holy, what we *see* is his glory – the *beauty* of holiness" (*ibid.*, emphasis his). *Holy* basically means set apart. Piper teaches: "God is *holy* means that God is in a class of perfection and greatness and value by himself. ...His holiness is his *utterly unique and perfect divine essence*" (*ibid.*, emphasis his). Therefore, placing holiness at the center of the definition says essentially the same thing as my basic definition above: the manifestation of His *Being* (which is holy). But the connection of glory as displayed holiness particularly enriches understanding in Scriptures like the quotation of Ezekiel 36:21-23 on page 42.

8.   See esp. "Hope of Glory," pp. 82-88.

9.   *The End for Which God Created the World*, ¶ 114, qtd. in John Piper, *God's Passion for His Glory: Living the Vision of Jonathan Edwards* (Wheaton, IL: Crossway, 1998), 33, where one can find many more glorious quotes from Edwards.

fame of God's Name. *Glory* and *name* are logically connected. *Glory* "suggests something which radiates from the one who has it, leaving an *impression* behind."[10] The manifestation of God's Being establishes a *reputation*, which is the significance of *name*.[11] A name is more than a word; it is a verbal marker to represent the whole person and his character. When we hear a name, we think of that person – and everything wrapped up in our memory and appraisal of him, that is, his reputation. Therefore, the revelation that God always acts for the sake of His great Name is another way of saying God always acts for His glory.[12]

God's Name is literally *Yahweh*, which is obscured in major English translations by small caps "Lord" or "God." The explanation for this unfortunate mistranslation, as well as the definition and importance of the word *Yahweh*, will be saved for *The Preeminence of Christ: Part Two, The I AM*.[13] Here we can simply say God explained the Name *Yahweh* as "I AM who I AM," with an apparent emphasis on His self-sufficient, sovereign presence to redeem and support.[14] At present, we will focus on the significance of the Name as the reputation and fame of the one true God, Yahweh.

God Himself defined His glory *as His* goodness *known in His* Name *(i.e., His reputation) for loving and judging*.[15] After Israel's golden calf idolatry and Moses' glory-of-God-motivated intercession which spared them, Moses asked God, "Please show

---

10. Sverre Aalen, "Glory, Honour," *NIDNT*, 2:44 (emphasis mine).

11. That *name* means *reputation* can be seen in Mark 6:14: "King Herod heard of it, for Jesus' *name* had become known...." Also, Revelation 3:1: "...You have the *reputation* [*onoma*] of being alive" is, literally, "You have the *name* of being alive." Cf. also Jer. 32:20, Dan. 9:15, Neh. 9:10.

12. E.g., *name, glory,* and *praise* are paralleled in Isaiah 48:9, 11.

13. Free at ProjectOne28.com/IAM.

14. See Ex. 3:12-22, 6:2-9, and the commentary in *Part Two,* particularly chapters one and three (free at ProjectOne28.com/IAM).

15. Thanks to Dr. James Hamilton, Jr., for drawing my attention to the significance of Ex. 33-34 as the definition of Yahweh's glory (*God's Glory in Salvation through Judgment*, 103).

me your glory" (Ex. 33:18). Moses asked to see God's *glory*, and therefore, God's answer is instructive:

> And He said, "I will make all my *goodness* pass before you and will proclaim before you my *name*, Yahweh. And I will be gracious to whom I will be gracious, and I will show mercy on whom I will show mercy. But," he said, "you cannot see my face, for man shall not see me and live." And Yahweh said, "Behold, there is a place by me where you shall stand on the rock, and while my *glory* passes by I will put you in a cleft of the rock, and I will cover you with my hand until I have passed by. Then I will take away my hand, and you shall see my back, but my face shall not be seen" (33:19-23).

Then, at the actual event:

> Yahweh descended in the cloud and stood with him there, and proclaimed the Name of Yahweh. Yahweh passed before him and proclaimed, "Yahweh, Yahweh, a God merciful and gracious, slow to anger, and abounding in steadfast love and faithfulness, keeping steadfast love for thousands, bearing[16] iniquity and transgression and sin, but who will by no means clear the guilty, visiting the iniquity of the fathers on the children and the children's children, to the third and the fourth generation." And Moses quickly bowed his head toward the earth and worshiped (34:5-8, AT).

Moses asked for *glory*, and God gave him a visual experience of His *goodness* and an audible experience of His *Name* and its accurate reputation (merciful and judging). Appropriately so, Moses worshiped. *God's glory, His self-revelation, resulted in praise.* This passage clearly shows who God is and what He does for His glory, and this passage "in turn profoundly influenced

---

16. The word translated as "forgiving" in all major translations is literally "bearing" or "carrying" (even "carrying off/away"). (Thanks, Christopher J. H. Wright, *Knowing God the Father Through the Old Testament* [Downers Grove, IL: IVP Academic, 2007], 32-33.) This is vital because it is the same word used later in Isaiah 53:12 about the Servant of Yahweh, Jesus: "...For He *bore* the sin of many and made intercession for the transgressors" (cf. 1 Pet. 2:24). The glory of Yahweh in Exodus 34:6-7 is the revelation that He Himself would bear judgment for our sin (in Jesus, *Yeshua*, meaning *Yahweh saves*) to save us by His compassion and steadfast love!

every other biblical author."[17] Therefore, we will return to it repeatedly to mine the depths of its riches.[18]

JEALOUSY

God not only wants love, worship, and glory from us – and rightfully so – but God is jealous for it. This is another difficult word for our minds to apply to God. Jealousy in humans carries a negative stigma. If I do not want another to receive recognition or reward because I want it for myself, then I am selfishly sinful.[19] But again, God is in a completely different category (holy, set apart, uniquely perfect). All things *are* from Him and through Him and *unto Him* (Rom. 11:36). Do not mistakenly think that God needs glory – or anything else (Acts 17:25, Ps. 50:12). He is *El Shaddai*, "God All-sufficient."[20] The simple truth is, now that things exist, the Creator God *deserves* everything that is His. Therefore, it is right for God to be jealous. The first two of the Ten Commandments demand sole allegiance. God prefaced them with His worth as the only God:

> *"I am Yahweh…* You shall have no other gods before me. You shall not make for yourself a carved image… You shall not bow down to them or serve them, *for I, Yahweh, am a jealous God…"* (Ex. 20:2-5).

Besides the infinite difference between God and Man, we must note that not all human jealousy is wrong. If a wife became smitten with another man, then her husband would be rightly provoked to jealousy because he loves her and deserves her faithful love. Our God is a jealous Husband.[21] When we cheat on Him and exchange His glory for a lesser thing, He burns with

---

17. Hamilton, 63. He also includes a helpful appendix, "Exodus 34:6-7 in the Law, Prophets, and Writings," on pp. 133-137.

18. See pp. 41, 46, 52 (n. 21), 55, 69, 74 (n. 9), 91. See also *Part Two*, 39, 120.

19. In fact, jealousy caused sinners to sell Joseph (Acts 7:9), oppose Moses (Ps. 106:16), try to kill David (1 Sam. 18:7-12), crucify Jesus (Mk. 15:10), and persecute the Church (Acts 5:17, 13:45, 17:5).

20. See n. 38 on p. 25.

jealousy.[22] In fact, the Spirit goes so far as to say God's Name is Jealous: "for you shall worship no other God, for *Yahweh, whose name is Jealous*, is a jealous God" (Ex. 34:14).

English Bibles often render translations that the "zeal" of God will accomplish something; it is the same Hebrew word also translated "jealousy."[23] God acts passionately out of jealousy for His glory, and He should. Because of this reality, God's servants – His *godly* ones – should be jealous for His sake, as were Phinehas (Num. 25:13), Elijah (1 Ki. 19:10, 14), Paul (2 Cor. 11:2), and Jesus (Ps. 69:19, Jn. 2:17). We should worship and serve God alone, and we should burn with desire for all to worship and serve Him alone.[24]

With this foundational understanding of *glory* and *name*, along with the common sense of who is most valuable, we can begin to examine the Scriptural testimony that God's greatest goal in all His works – from beginning to end – is His glory in the preeminence of His Son.

---

21. See, e.g., Isa. 54:5-8, 64:4-5, Ezek. 16:4 ff. (esp. vv. 32, 38), Jer. 31:32, Hos. 2:14-16. Cf. *Part Two*, 103.

22. Jer. 2:11, Rom. 1:21-23, qtd. on p. 10. Also, Jas. 4:4 (NIV, cf. fn. 24 below).

23. E.g., Isa. 9:7. Leonard J. Coppes (*TWOT*, 802) writes, "This verb expresses a very strong emotion whereby some quality or possession of the object is desired by the subject.... It may prove helpful to think of 'zeal' as the original sense from which derived the notions 'zeal for another's property' = 'envy' and 'zeal for one's own property' = 'jealousy.'" Precisely my point, since glory (and all things) are truly the Creator's own property (Ps. 24:1; 1 Chron. 29:10-14; Rom. 11:36). See also n. 74 on p. 40 concerning "jealousy" in the exile, judgment, and restoration.

24. Consider the literal 2 Cor. 11:29: "Who is stumbled, and I do not inwardly burn?" Cf. Zeph. 1:18, "the fire of his jealousy" (cf. 3:8), and, "zeal for your house has consumed me" (Ps. 69:9, Jn. 2:17, i.e., "eaten me up like a fire," cf. Ps. 119:139).

CHAPTER ONE

GOD'S WORKS PURPOSED FOR HIS GLORY

In this opening chapter, we will survey Old Testament history to demonstrate its pervasive theme: God's ultimate purpose in all of His works is the glory of His Name. God repeatedly reveals this, not only in reflections on the past or propositions for the present, but often in promises of future grace, which Chapter Two will show are ultimately fulfilled in His Son. We can rightly understand the gospel (or anything) only if we see how it relates to God's glory as taught in Scripture, so we now commence an essential study.

CREATION

Why did God create the heavens and the earth? In disciple-making sessions, we often hear answers such as "for us to live here," which seem indicative of the church's popular man-centered theology. In truth, God created all physical things, angels, and Man for His glory.

Things. "At creation Yahweh designed a cosmic theater for his glory."[1] According to Psalm 19:1, "The heavens declare the glory of God, and the sky above proclaims his handiwork." The physical world truly cries out that it has been created by a powerful, majestic, beautiful, wise God. "For since the creation of the world His invisible attributes are clearly seen, being understood by the things that are made, even His eternal power and Godhead…" (Rom. 1:20 NKJV). Physical creation manifests God, in other words, displays His glory.[2]

The created things themselves "praise" God (e.g., Ps. 148:3-10), and we respond at the sight of them with our own praise to God. For example,[3] Psalm 104 marvels at God's sovereignty in stretching out the heavens, laying the foundations of the earth, rebuking the abyss and raising the mountains, gushing forth springs, growing trees and grass, feeding His creatures, and revolving the sun and moon. Therefore, the psalmist overflows:

> How manifold are Your works, Yahweh! In wisdom You have made them all…. May the glory of Yahweh endure forever; may Yahweh rejoice in His works…. I will sing praise to my God while I have being…. Bless Yahweh, my soul! Praise Yah! (104:24, 31, 33, 35, AT).

With a view to Christ's preeminence under this overarching purpose of God's glory, it should be stated that God created all things *through* Christ and *for* Christ. John 1:3 speaks of Jesus, whose eternal, pre-incarnate Name was "the Word"[4]: "Through him all things were made; without him nothing was made that has been made" (NIV). God the Father willed Creation, and the Word was His creative agent. In Genesis 1:3 and following, "And God *said*…. And God *said*…," represents the Word in action (cf. Gen. 1:6, 7; Heb. 11:3; 2 Pet. 3:5).

---

1. Hamilton, *God's Glory in Salvation through Judgment*, 50.

2. For fuller treatment of creation as speech, dramatizing the spiritual into the physical realm, see *Light Shines in the Darkness*, free at ProjectOne28.com.

3. Thanks to Thomas R. Schreiner, "A Biblical Theology of the Glory of God," in *For the Fame of God's Name: Essays in Honor of John Piper*, ed. Sam Storms and Justin Taylor (Wheaton, IL: Crossway, 2010), 216-217.

4. See more on the Name "Word" in Chapter Two, 45-46, and *Part Two,* 117-118.

Not only have all things been created *through* Christ, but also *for* Christ. Colossians 1:16 reveals that "all things have been created through Him and for Him" (AT). As Creator, the Father is the owner of all things, and He desires to give all things to His Son as an inheritance (e.g., Heb. 1:2). To teach that God created all things for His glory and for Christ is not a contradiction if we distinguish subordinate means and the ultimate end. By giving stewardship of creation to the Son (means), God will be glorified (end). I officially have jumped ahead of myself since "Heir of all things" will be covered in the last installment in this series, Lord willing. But He is worth it!

Angels. Among creation, angels hold a unique place as worshipers and servants for the sake of God's glory. They were created before the earth, animals, and Man, and they sang joyful worship songs to God when He laid the foundation of the earth (Job 38:4-7). In fact, angels never cease worshiping God around His throne, crying, "Holy, holy, holy is the Lord God Almighty, who was and is and is to come!" (Rev. 4:8, cf. Isa. 6:3). We noted earlier that God receives glory because of creation. Now we can see[5] that every time the four living creatures (angels) cry, "Holy, holy, holy," the twenty-four elders (angels)[6] fall down and "give glory and honor" to God (Rev. 4:9-10) *specifically for being the Creator:* "Worthy are you, our Lord and God, to receive glory and honor and power, for you created all things, and by your will they existed and were created" (4:11).

Good angels do only what God commands, so we see God's priority in their activity. Good angels sing of God's glory and worth, which shows God's desire to be worshiped. Indeed, Psalm 29 commands the angels: "Ascribe to Yahweh, sons of God, ascribe to Yahweh glory and strength. *Ascribe to Yahweh the*

---

5. Thanks to Schreiner, *op. cit.*, 217-218.

6. Some believe these elders are human representatives, but the elders sing about the redeemed as "they," not "we" (Rev. 5:10), which shows they are angelic. The inferior textual evidence for KJV's rendering of "us" and "we" cannot be correct because then

glory due His Name…" (vv. 1-2, AT). The psalm continues, in a polemic against the Canaanite storm god Baal,[7] to credit Yahweh with sovereignty over a storm in Canaan. The scene begins in verse 3 by calling Yahweh "the God of glory" and concludes in verse 9 (AT) with angelic response to Yahweh's voice in the storm: "in His [heavenly[8]] temple everyone is saying, 'Glory!'" That's just what angels are in the habit of doing – exclaiming that Yahweh has glory. We should join them.

Man. Scripture speaks of only one creature as being made in the image of God: Man. Genesis 1:26-28 (AT) reads:

> [26]And God said, "Let Us make Man in Our image, according to Our likeness, so that they may rule over the fish of the sea and over the birds of the heavens and over the cattle and over all the earth and over all the crawlers crawling on the earth."

> [27]And God created Man in His image;
> in the image of God He created him;
> male and female He created them.

> [28]And God blessed them, and God said to them, "Be fruitful and multiply, and fill the earth, and subdue it, and rule over the fish of the sea and over the birds of the heavens and over every living thing crawling on the earth."

Special among all creation, Man is purposed *to show what God is like*, which is language similar to *manifesting God's glory*. Psalm 8, which is commentary on Genesis 1:26-28, opens with Yahweh's transcendence: "You have set your glory above the heavens" (v. 1). Then our Lord's immanence appears through His care for Man whom He has crowned with glory and honor

---

the four living creatures (co-singers here, 5:8, and clearly angelic, 4:6-8) would be redeemed, too. These elders must be angels who rule in kingly fashion.

7. See Allen P. Ross, *A Commentary on the Psalms*, Vol. 1 (1-41), KEL (Grand Rapids, MI: Kregel, 2011), 653, 656, 658.

8. Ross reasons, "'Temple' here probably refers to the heavenly temple, because the use of 'glory' recalls the beginning of the psalm where the angelic hosts were enjoined to give God the glory" (*ibid.*, 661).

(royal terms, v. 5).[9] The apostle Paul joins the concepts of image and glory in 1 Corinthians 11:7, teaching that Man "*is* the image and glory of God." Man was created not simply *for* the glory of God; Man was created *to be* the glory of God!

It is actually quite tricky to pin down what it is about Man that comprises the image of God. Scripture does not break this down categorically.[10] Therefore, some teachers focus solely on the function of Man as what images forth God's likeness. In context, the purposed function is ruling (Gen. 1:26, 28). However, it seems that the grammar[11] and logic should be clear that God's image is what we *are*, and what we *are* as God's image enables us *to do* the function of ruling.[12] That is to say, because Man is the Creator's "son,"[13] Man's nature is uniquely capable of relating to God the Father. Man can receive the spiritual realities of God, process them with God-like reason, emotions, and will, and then incarnate them into the physical realm with speech and action – glory, the "going public" of God's goodness.[14]

---

9. "...care for him" is lit., "that You visit him" (Ross, 295, also n. 19).

10. John Piper, "The Image of God: An Approach from Biblical and Systematic Theology." *Studia Biblica et Theologica* 1:1 (March 1971), available at desiringGod. org/articles/the-image-of-god. For more on Man as God's image, see ProjectOne28. com/image.

11. "The sequence of verbs in [Gen. 1] v. 26 is inadequately represented in most modern translations.... grammarians of Hebrew agree that this particular sequence marks purpose or result. The correct translation, therefore, is 'let us make man... *so that* they may rule.' ...the ruling is not the essence of the divine image, but rather a result of being made as the divine image" (Peter J. Gentry, "Kingdom through Covenant: Humanity as the Divine Image," *SBJT* 12/1 [2008]: 25, emphasis his).

12. Gentry, *ibid.*, 25, 32. G. K. Beale, *A New Testament Biblical Theology: The Unfolding of the Old Testament in the New* (Grand Rapids, MI: Baker Academic, 2011), 30-32; Piper (n. 8, above). The image must be *ontological*, because sinners – who have rebelled against the *functional* role of filling the earth with God's glory and government – are still considered to be in God's image and likeness (Gen. 9:6; 1 Cor. 11:7; Jas. 3:9). If the imaging was solely functional, sinners would not be God's image after the Fall. For more, see ProjectOne28.com/image, which draws from these scholars.

13. Peter J. Gentry & Stephen J. Wellum emphasize the covenantal father/son relationship inferred, in the ancient Near East, by the word "likeness" (*God's Kingdom through God's Covenants: A Concise Biblical Theology* [Wheaton, IL: Crossway, 2015], 76-77, 79-80). See Lk. 3:38, which calls Adam the son of God.

In the Egyptian and Mesopotamian context in which Israel received Genesis, the foreign kings were images of their false gods.[15] The king was a "living statue" made to resemble and represent the god's presence and power over his territory.[16] In truth, however, all humans are images of the one real God. All humans are purposed to be God's royal representatives who manifest His character in benevolent dominion. Therefore, God empowered[17] and commissioned Man to be fruitful, multiply, fill, subdue, and rule (Gen. 1:28). God wanted to fill the earth *with image-bearers* in order to fill the earth *with His glory* (cf. Num. 14:21, Hab. 2:14). Faithful image-bearers in every part of the earth could subdue the enemy and the wasteland by the blessing of God, thereby extending the Garden of Eden so that the whole earth could be a suitable dwelling place for the God of glory.[18]

We can become so accustomed to the teaching about Man in God's image that we lose our sense of its strangeness. Most often in the Hebrew Scriptures, "image" is used of idols! Yahweh expressly forbade His people from crafting images of Him, idols, because He had already made His images – us![19] We are God's (appropriate) idols! Piper asks well:

> What would it mean if you were to create seven billion statues of yourself and put them all over the world? It would mean you would want people to notice you! God created us in His

14. See *Spirit, Soul, Body: The Blueprint of Man in God's Image*, free at ProjectOne28. com. See also ProjectOne28.com/image.

15. Beale, *A New Testament Biblical Theology*, 31; Gentry, 26-30.

16. Gentry, 27 (see ProjectOne28.com/image).

17. John N. Oswalt defines the Hebrew behind "blessed" (Gen. 1:28): "to endue with power for success, prosperity, fecundity, longevity, etc." (*"bārak," TWOT*, 132).

18. Cf. Gen. 3:8 with Rev. 21:3. See G. K. Beale, *The Temple and the Church's Mission: A Biblical Theology of the Dwelling Place of God*, ed. D. A. Carson (Downers Grove, IL: InterVarsity Press, 2004). See also Sam McVay, Jr., and Spencer Stewart, *Introduction to Disciple-making: Obeying the Global Mandate of the Resurrected King Jesus* (El Dorado, KS: Project one28, 2013), 30-31 (free at ProjectOne28.com/i2dm).

19. Ex. 20:4-5 in light of Gen. 1:26-27

image so we would display or reflect or communicate who He is, how great He is, and what He's like.[20]

Our very existence is preeminently about God. We are purposed to always think, feel, speak, and act in a way that directs everyone's attention to the glory of God the King.

SIN IN THE CONTEXT OF GLORY

I submit that everything should be considered in connection with God's glory, including sin. Satan began as a perfect angel, created to glorify God, but he rejected the matchlessness of God's glory and sought his own.[21] Satan's prideful rebellion was the prototype for Man, whom he tempted.[22] The worst result of Adam and Eve's sin was that they stopped fully displaying the glory of God and began propagating a species of glory-deniers.

Romans 1 penetratingly breaks down the nature of sin. All mankind "knew God" through the display of His glory in creation (1:19-21). However, "they did not approve of having God in their knowledge" (1:28, AT). We did not *want* an obedience-demanding, glory-deserving God to rule over us. Therefore, in rebellious disbelief, we suppressed the truth of God through unrighteousness (1:18), and we "did not glorify Him as God or give thanks" (1:21, AT). *The essence of sin is refusing to glorify God.*

The inevitable next step is choosing a substitute because we are wired to be glorifiers. Not worshiping is not an option. Therefore, sinners "*exchanged the glory of the immortal God* for a likeness of an image of mortal man and birds and four-footed animals and crawling things" (1:23, AT). *Idolatry* means "idol worship." Modern Americans fancy themselves more

---

20. John Piper, "What Does It Mean to Be Made in God's Image?" Ask Pastor John, Episode 153, 19 Aug 2013 (desiringGod.org/interviews/what-does-it-mean-to-be-made-in-god-s-image).

21. Isa. 14:12-15, Ezek. 28:12-19; see *Light Shines in the Darkness* (ProjectOne28.com).

22. Gen. 3:1 ff., cf. 1 Tim. 3:6

sophisticated than primitive fetish fanatics. But we have all worshiped the image in the mirror, exchanging the glory of God in pursuit of glory for self, have we not? For this, "the wrath of God is being manifested" (1:18, AT).

Paul may have been basing his glory-exchange teaching on Jeremiah 2:11-13.[23] That prophetic word shows the shocking ugliness of sin, which is, by nature, two-sided:

> Has a nation changed its gods,
>   even though they are no gods?
> But my people have *changed their glory*
>   for that which does not profit.
> Be appalled, O heavens, at this;
>   be shocked, be utterly desolate,
>   declares Yahweh,
> for my people have committed two evils:
> they have forsaken me,
>   the fountain of living waters,
> and hewed out cisterns for themselves,
>   broken cisterns that can hold no water.

Sin first denies God's glory and then prefers some lesser thing.[24] How foolish can we be? We forsake the all-sufficient source of life and joy ("the fountain of living waters") for busted knock-offs that cannot satisfy ("broken cisterns that can hold no water"). Only the glory of Yahweh can satisfy image-bearers, but in the betrayal of the ages, we exchanged it and now treasure lesser creations above our Creator.

The glory-redirecting nature of sin was plainly exposed at the Tower of Babel when men refused to fill the earth for God's glory and instead rallied to build one city and heavenly tower (Gen.

---

23. Also Ps. 106:20. Cf. Douglas J. Moo, *The Epistle to the Romans*, NICNT (Grand Rapids, MI: Eerdmans, 1996), 108-109.

24. See John Piper, "Sin Prefers Anything to God," Ask Pastor John, Episode 570, 8 Apr 2015 (desiringGod.org/interviews/sin-prefers-anything-to-god); *idem.*, "What Is Sin? The Essence and Root of All Sinning," 2 Feb 2015 (desiringGod.org/messages/the-origin-essence-and-definition-of-sin).

11:1-4). They clearly stated their motivation: "...and let us make a name for ourselves" (11:4). Sinners want glory for themselves instead of for God. Therefore, God brought judgment upon the Man-glorifying project at Babel, as He always will. As another example, King Herod, receiving glory for self, was struck dead by an angel of the Lord "because he did not give God the glory" (Acts 12:23).

Romans 3:23 says "all sinned and are lacking the glory of God" (AT). I first thought of *glory* as meaning "standard" – Man failed to live up to God's standard and expectation, and so sin consigns us to hell instead of heaven. Now I believe its meaning is much deeper: Man abdicated his God-designed destiny to *be* the glory of God, to shine forth His goodness and government in all the earth. The greatest crime and tragedy of sin is not the consequence for Man, but the glory denied to God by our exchanging it for lesser treasures (cf. 1:21-23). As we will see in Chapters Three and Four, that is why God's motivation for salvation and His holy ones' pleas for forgiveness are based upon concern for God's glory. Here in Romans 3:23, flowing from Paul's analysis in 1:21-23, we see that glory-deniers are glory-lackers. Only glory-givers become glory-filled.

WAR OVER GOD'S GLORY IN JOB

Chapters one and two of Job reveal the book's main point to be the spiritual war between God and Satan over the glory of God.[25] Satan slandered the worth of God and challenged that God is not valuable enough that Job would still worship Him after losing everything (1:8-11). Satan claimed Job really only loved the blessings; he did not love God simply for being God. And God decided to show His worth through Job's faith (1:12). Job lost his oxen, donkeys, sheep, servants, seven sons, and three daughters on the same day (1:13-19). We have not

---

25. This section is adapted from "Trusting God Is Good When Bad Happens," 26 Jun 2011, as well as notes from my OT Survey class at Veritas (ProjectOne28.com/Job).

properly studied this book until we read that section slowly, imagine being in his shoes, and just weep. Job later said that God would not let him catch his breath (9:18). The heartache was suffocating. And yet, consider his response:

> Then Job arose and tore his robe and shaved his head and fell on the ground and *worshiped*. And he said, "Naked I came from my mother's womb, and naked shall I return. Yahweh gave, and Yahweh has taken away; *blessed be the Name of Yahweh*." In all this Job did not sin or charge God with wrong (1:20-22).

God then boasted in Job's worshipful victory over Satan (2:3). But Satan again slandered the worth of God and challenged God that He is not valuable enough that Job would love Him more than health and life itself (2:4-5). And God decided to show His worth through Job's faith; Satan was given permission to strike Job with loathsome sores from head to toe (2:6-8, cf. 7:5). Yet Job still trusted that God was sovereign and good (2:9-10). As months of suffering passed (7:3), Job began to despair and then to try to understand why God would allow this. He spoke things that charged God with injustice,[26] and God appeared to him in the whirlwind to rebuke and correct (chs. 38-41).

Then Job retracted his rebellious statements, admitted he had not known God well enough, confessed his ignorance of God's ways, and asserted renewed confidence in God's absolute sovereignty (42:1-6). What is so vital to see is that Job literally said, "...I am *comforted* in dust and ashes" (42:6). Popularly (and plausibly) translated here as "repent," this Hebrew word most commonly means "comforted," which is how it is translated in all six other uses in this book in development as a major theme.[27]

---

26. E.g., 27:2. Cf. 33:9-12, 40:2, 8.

27. Job 2:11, 7:13, 16:2, 21:34, 29:25, 42:11 (see biblestudytools.com/lexicons/hebrew/nas/nacham.html). Add 42:6 to equal seven – a significant number for this key theme. Notice the ESV translation footnote to 42:6 and the *ESV Study Bible* note, as well as the "Literary Features" section to the book's Introduction. Cf. *TWOT*, 570-571. G. K. Chesterton wrote: "...God comes in at the end, not to

Job was "comforted" in the presence of God *before* being healed – and in that state, God's glory was demonstrated victoriously against Satan's slander!

In the beginning and at the end, Job's faith defeated the enemy by giving glory to God. This is why we were created:

> Out of the mouth of babies and infants,
> you have established strength because of your foes,
> to still the enemy and the avenger (Ps. 8:2).

Jesus quoted the Greek "translation" of this Hebrew verse ("ordained praise" in Mt. 21:16 versus "established strength" in Ps. 8:2). He thus endorsed the interpretation that what comes out of our mouths to stop the enemy is *praise*.[28] Our giving glory to God overcomes the slander of God's enemy. This is why we were created and why we were re-created in Christ. Ephesians 3:10 says God planned before the ages to save Jews and Gentiles in Christ, "in order that the manifold wisdom of God may now be made known to the rulers and the authorities in the heavenly realms through the Assembly."[29]

May we "consider… Job" and assemble on the battle lines in this war over God's glory with unflinching trust in His good purposes for our every trial (Jas. 5:10-11).

ISRAEL FOR THE GLORY OF HIS NAME

Out of the carnage of the Flood and the confusion of Babel, God called Abram out of Babylon to create a nation that would restore the Genesis 1:28 blessing to all the families of the earth

---

answer riddles, but to propound them. …which makes Job suddenly satisfied with the mere presentation of something impenetrable. Verbally speaking the enigmas of Jehovah seem darker and more desolate than the enigmas of Job; yet Job was comfortless before the speech of Jehovah and is comforted after it. He has been told nothing, but he feels the terrible and tingling atmosphere of something which is too good to be told. The refusal of God to explain His design is itself a burning hint of His design. The riddles of God are more satisfying than the solutions of man" ("Introduction to the Book of Job," chesterton.org/introduction-to-job, par. 10).

28. See the author's ProjectOne28.com/psalm8 for more commentary.

(Gen. 12:1-3). Though Abram was old and childless, he gave glory to God, trusting God was able to fulfill His promise (Rom. 4:20-21). God purposed that Abram's descendants would receive His truth and manifest it, walking in "the way of Yahweh by doing righteousness and justice" (Gen. 18:19). These descendants would constitute a great nation called Israel, to whom Yahweh said, "You shall be to me a kingdom of priests and a holy nation" (Ex. 19:6).[30] As a kingdom, Israel would gladly receive the kingship which Yahweh truly expresses over all the earth. As priests, Israel would worship and teach[31] the other nations to also give glory to the only true God, Yahweh. As a holy nation, Israel would receive and submit to God's Law in order to *show* Him holy[32] (i.e., *glorify* Him). In Isaiah 43:7, Yahweh prophesies of His redeemed people as "everyone who is called by my name, whom I created for my glory." Jeremiah 13:11 likewise reveals God's purpose in forming Israel: *"that they might be for me a people, a name, a praise, and a glory."*

THE EXODUS FOR THE GLORY OF HIS NAME

God indeed multiplied Abram's descendants, but because Satan hates the glory of God in image-bearers, the Pharaoh in Egypt oppressed the Israelites and murdered their baby boys (Ex. 1:8-22, cf. Jn. 8:44, Gen. 3:15). The survival of Israel and the fulfillment of God's promise would require a miraculous deliverance by the hand of God. The Exodus was the first event in the Bible described as redemption,[33] and it became *the* prototype

---

29. Lit. That Ephesians 3:10 speaks of us showing God's wisdom to His *angelic* enemy is evident by the parallel language in 6:12 about dark, evil rulers and authorities.

30. Cf. 1 Pet. 2:5, 9; Rev. 1:6, 5:10, 20:6 for application to the new covenant Church.

31. Lev. 10:11; Deut. 31:9-13, 33:10; Hos. 4:1-4; Ezek. 44:23; e.g., Ps. 96:3, 10. Christopher J. H. Wright, "Who Are We and What Are We Here For? The Identity and Calling of God's People," AGTS Spring Lectureship, 21 Jan 2010 (http://www.agts.edu/news/news_archives/2010_1_19spring_lectureship.html).

32. E.g., Lev. 11:44-45, 19:2, 20:7, 20:26. For the connection between showing God as holy and glorifying Him, see n. 7 on p. 7.

33. Christopher J. H. Wright in n. 31 above.

for salvation. The nation looked back to it as the foundation of their existence and present security,[34] and the prophets looked forward to a new exodus, new covenant, and new creation.[35] That "new thing" (Isa. 42:1-9) was achieved by Christ. On the Mount of Transfiguration, Moses and Elijah spoke with Jesus "of *His exodus*, which He was about to accomplish at Jerusalem" (Lk. 9:31, AT). This underscores the value for us, as new covenant Christians, in understanding God's goal in the original Exodus: it was the precedent for Jesus' exodus, His resurrection and ascension after dying as the ultimate Passover Lamb (more on pp. 30-31).

Yahweh saved Israel from Egypt for the glory of His Name. From the beginning, God declared to Moses His intention to make His Name known through this deliverance. He did so by explaining His Name in Exodus 3:14-15[36] and by what 6:2-3 reports:[37]

> And God spoke to Moses, and said to him: "*I am Yahweh. And I showed myself to Abraham, to Isaac, and to Jacob in the character of El Shaddai,*[38] *but in the character expressed by my name Yahweh I did not make myself known to them.*"

---

34. E.g., Hos. 2:15, 13:4; Mic. 6:3-4; Isa. 50:2

35. E.g., Isa. 10:24-27, 11:6-8, 11:15-16, 32:15, 43:2, 43:16-21, 48:20-21, 51:3, 52:11-12; Mic. 2:12-13, 4:10; Jer. 16:14-21, 31:31-33; Hos. 12:9; Hab. 3:1-15; Ezek. 36:35. In fact, passages such as Jer. 16:14-16 and Isa. 11:10-16 anticipated the new exodus would be greater than the original ("Session 7: The Exile and the Prophetic Promises," ProjectOne28.com/HIStory).

36. See *Part Two*, Chapter One, "Yahweh in Exodus 3" (ProjectOne28.com/IAM).

37. Translation by J. A. Motyer in "The Revelation of the Divine Name" (available free at TheologicalStudies.org.uk/article_revelation_motyer.html). This verse cannot mean, as liberal scholars take it, that the forefathers did not know at all the Name *Yahweh*, because as early as Adam's grandson (in the lifetime of Adam), they were calling upon the Name of Yahweh (Gen. 4:26). They did not know Him in the character of that Name: the God present to redeem through judgment. Motyer made my heart burn within me at the close of his article, teaching the closest the forefathers came to this knowledge was the only time the Name was expounded: when God provided the lamb to redeem Isaac, Abraham called Him *Yahweh-Yireh*, meaning *Yahweh provides*. What a foreshadow of the Exodus and of Christ! See *Part Two*, pp. 31-35, for more.

38. Hebrew for "God All-sufficient," traditionally translated "God Almighty" because of

Yahweh purposed this event to reveal the glory of His Name (in redemption through judgment, Ex. 34:6-7) in ways that had not been experienced by the forefathers. He announced:

> "…I have remembered My covenant. Say therefore to the people of Israel, 'I am Yahweh, and I will bring you out from under the burdens of the Egyptians, and I will deliver you from slavery to them, and I will redeem you with an outstretched arm and with great acts of judgment. I will take you to be My people, and I will be your God, and *you shall know that I am Yahweh* your God…" (6:5-7).

God closed the speech as He opened it: *"I am Yahweh"* (6:8). Later, God related His purpose for future generations of Israel also to know His glory: "that you may tell in the hearing of your son and of your grandson how I have dealt harshly with the Egyptians and what signs I have done among them, *that you may know that I am Yahweh"* (10:2).

Pharaoh had made a foolish, defiant response at Moses' first visit: "Who is Yahweh, that I should obey His voice and let Israel go? I do not know Yahweh…" (5:2). Therefore, God repeatedly declared His intention to teach Pharaoh by showing His glory:

- *"I am Yahweh;* tell Pharaoh king of Egypt all that I say to you" (6:29).

- "by this you shall *know that I am Yahweh"* (7:17)

- "that you may *know that there is no one like Yahweh"* (8:10)

- "that you may *know that I, Yahweh, am in the land"* (8:22)

- "For this time I will send all my plagues on you yourself, and on your servants and your people, so that you may *know that there is none like me in all the earth"* (9:14).

---

the Greek translation (*pantokratōr*). However, the Hebrew *shadday* means "enough" (*TWOT*, 907). Singling out power seems unnecessarily limiting when every attribute of God is "enough." He is totally all-sufficient. I must submit, though, to the fact that the NT continues the LXX translation, Almighty (e.g., Rev. 4:8, 11:17, 15:3).

- "so that you may *know that the earth is Yahweh's"* (9:29)

- "that you may *know that Yahweh makes a distinction* between Egypt and Israel" (11:7)

We should take care to remember our struggle is not against flesh and blood, but against God's demonic enemy (Eph. 6:12). Explaining the final judgment and the Passover, God said, "… *on all the gods* of Egypt I will execute judgments. *I am Yahweh"* (Ex. 12:12, cf. Num. 33:4). Each of the ten plagues showed Yahweh's power over an Egyptian false god,[39] and the final judgment exposed them all as completely worthless. Pharaoh considered himself an incarnation of the gods, and so he bore specific judgment.

God raised up Pharaoh for the very purpose of gaining glory for Himself through the proclamation of His Name:

> "But for this purpose I have raised you up, to show you my power, *so that my name may be proclaimed in all the earth"* (Ex. 9:16, cf. Rom. 9:17).

> "And I will strengthen[40] Pharaoh's heart, and he will pursue them, and *I will get glory* over Pharaoh and all his host, and the Egyptians shall *know that I am Yahweh"* (Ex. 14:4, AT).

> "And I will strengthen the hearts of the Egyptians so that they shall go in after them, and *I will get glory* over Pharaoh and all his host, his chariots, and his horsemen. [18]And the Egyptians shall *know that I am Yahweh, when I have gotten glory* over Pharaoh, his chariots, and his horsemen" (14:17-18, AT).

Those two latest Scriptures show God purposed that the Egyptians, too, should know His glory, as also stated earlier in the narrative:

---

39. See ProjectOne28.com/plagues.

40. I was first taught that God hardened Pharaoh's heart only after Pharaoh hardened his own heart. I now see that the Scriptural data is more complex than that – and it matters for the glory of Yahweh's Name. See "The Hardening of Pharaoh (and Millions of Others)" at ProjectOne28.com/hardening.

"But I will make difficult Pharaoh's heart, and *so that I may multiply My signs and wonders* in the land of Egypt, [4]Pharaoh will not listen to you. Then I will lay My hand on Egypt and bring My hosts, My people the children of Israel, out of the land of Egypt by great acts of judgment. [5]The Egyptians shall *know that I am Yahweh*, when I stretch out My hand against Egypt and bring out the people of Israel from among them" (7:3-5, AT).

Needless to say, God's plan succeeded. Through the judgments and salvation of the Exodus, God was glorified, and Israel, Pharaoh, and the Egyptians came to know that Yahweh is the only true God.

Exodus 12:38 reports, "A mixed multitude also went up with them...." Traditionally, this has been interpreted as some Egyptians turning to faith in Yahweh and joining Israel's Exodus because of His signs and wonders.[41] Why stay in the ruined country that is an enemy of the one true God? Why not join those blessed by Him? Yahweh desired to be glorified by the Egyptians, and He was.

Yahweh also desired to be glorified by Israel, and He was. After Israel were delivered through the parted Red Sea, they worshiped in song:

> I will sing to Yahweh, for he has triumphed gloriously;
>   the horse and his rider he has thrown into the sea.
> Yah is my strength and my song,
>   and he has become my salvation;
> this is my God, and I will praise him,
>   my father's God, and I will exalt him.
> Yahweh is a man of war;
>   *Yahweh is his name* (15:1-3).

---

41. "Also...with them" indicates they were not part of Israel. John I. Durham writes, "That there were many who became Israelite by theological rather than biological descendancy is many times referred to in the OT and is the occasion for such requirements as those set forth in vv 43-49," regarding the integration of foreigners into Israel and her feasts (*Exodus*, WBC [Nashville: Thomas Nelson, 1987], 172).

Your right hand, O Yahweh, glorious in power,
> Your right hand, O Yahweh, shatters the enemy.
In the greatness of Your majesty You overthrow Your
> adversaries… (15:6-7).

Who is like You, O Yahweh, among the gods?
> Who is like You, majestic in holiness,
> awesome in glorious deeds, doing wonders? (15:11)

Yahweh will reign forever and ever (15:18).

What is more, Yahweh desired that His Name be proclaimed in all the earth, and it was (cf. Ex. 15:14-16). When "Jethro, the priest of Midian, Moses' father-in-law, heard of all that God had done…" (Ex. 18:1), he "rejoiced" and said, *"Blessed be Yahweh…. Now I know that Yahweh is greater than all gods…"* (18:9-11). Likewise, Rahab, a Canaanite prostitute miles away and a generation later, testified to the two Israelite spies:

> *"I know that Yahweh* has given you the land, and that the fear of you has fallen upon us, and that all the inhabitants of the land melt away before you. [10]*For we have heard how Yahweh* dried up the water of the Red Sea before you when you came out of Egypt, and what you did to the two kings of the Amorites who were beyond the Jordan, to Sihon and Og, whom you devoted to destruction. [11]And as soon as we heard it, our hearts melted, and there was no spirit left in any man because of you, for *Yahweh your God, he is God in the heavens above and on the earth beneath"* (Josh. 2:9-11).

Rahab turned from false gods to Yahweh, and by faith she, along with her family, was saved when Yahweh destroyed Jericho (Josh. 6:22-25). Not only that, but Rahab became an ancestor to King David (Mt. 1:5), honored in the family tree of King Jesus!

God wanted glory through the Exodus from future generations (10:2), and He got it. The psalmist remembered:

> Our fathers, when they were in Egypt,
> > did not consider your wondrous works;

they did not remember the abundance of your steadfast love,
    but rebelled by the sea, at the Red Sea.
Yet he saved them for his name's sake,
    that he might *make known* his mighty power....
Then they believed his words;
    they sang his *praise* (Ps. 106:7-8, 12).

Isaiah also remembered that Yahweh "caused his glorious arm to go at the right hand of Moses, who divided the waters before them *to make for himself an everlasting name.... So you led your people, to make for yourself a glorious name"* (63:12, 14). Jeremiah and Daniel in the exile and then the Levites after the restoration also declared in prayer that God had *made a Name for Himself* through the Exodus;[42] that is, He established a glorious reputation.

THE MOTIVATION FOR ISRAEL'S EXODUS AND FOR CHRIST'S EXODUS

Remember that the original exodus served as the great foreshadow of the "exodus" Jesus accomplished at Jerusalem (Lk. 9:31, lit.). Multiple parallels exist between Moses and Jesus and their deliverances.[43] God said of Israel's Exodus in Hosea 11:1, "Out of Egypt I called my son" (speaking of Israel as His son, cf. Ex. 4:22-23, Jer. 31:9). After Jesus' birth, His family fled to Egypt to escape Herod, the Roman "King of the Jews" who murdered the Jewish babies, just as Moses providentially escaped Pharaoh's genocide.[44] After Herod's death, Jesus came out of Egypt and into Israel, a move which Matthew taught was a fulfillment of the awaited new exodus: "This was to fulfill what the Lord had spoken by the prophet: 'Out of Egypt I called my son'" (Mt. 2:15). Jesus, God's true Son, is the fulfillment of God's desires for Israel,[45] and as God's Son, "Jesus has been counted worthy of more glory than Moses" (Heb. 3:3 ff.).

---

42. Jer. 32:20, Dan. 9:15, Neh. 9:10

43. In fulfillment of Deut. 18:15-18; cf. Acts 3:22 and context.

Yahweh redeemed Israel from Egypt by the atoning sacrifice of the Passover Lamb (Ex. 12). Israel's firstborn sons deserved the wrath of God, just as the Egyptians' did. Yet when Israel spread the blood of the lamb over their doorposts, the death of the substitute satisfied God's wrath, and God passed over them. Then when Jesus appeared, John the Baptist proclaimed, "Behold, the Lamb of God who takes away the sin of the world" (Jn. 1:29, cf. 1:36). The apostles Peter and Paul also called Jesus our pure, spotless Passover Lamb.[46]

In Exodus, Yahweh brought judgment on all the gods of Egypt; through God's judgment of sin upon Christ, Jesus condemned and triumphed over the devil and his demonic authorities.[47] Through the first exodus, God freed His people from slavery to Pharaoh; through Jesus' exodus, God freed His people from slavery to sin, Satan, and death. Israel's Passover led to the establishing of the (old) covenant, whereas Jesus shed His blood on Passover to establish the new covenant.[48]

Thus the Exodus served as a model for redemption through Christ. God's motivation for the Exodus was also His motivation for the Cross and Resurrection: the glory of His Name. We will see those explicit Scriptures beginning on page 54.

FOR THE SAKE OF GLORY IN THE WILDERNESS

To lead Israel out of Egypt, the *glory* of Yahweh manifested in a cloud by day and a pillar of fire by night.[49] In the wilderness,

---

44. Mt. 2:13-16, Ex. 1, Rev. 12:4-6

45. Many more examples of Christ as true Israel are cited in my "Introduction to the Old Testament" (ProjectOne28.com/OTsurvey).

46. 1 Pet. 1:19, 1 Cor. 5:7, cf. Jn. 19:31-37

47. Ex. 12:12; Rom. 6:7, 22, 8:2-3; Rev. 1:5; Heb. 2:14-15; 2 Tim. 1:10; Col. 2:15; Jn. 12:31, 16:11; 1 Jn. 3:8

48. Ex. 24:8, Heb. 9:19-20; Jn. 19:14; Lk. 22:20, Heb. 9:11-28, 12:24

49. Ex. 13:21, 14:19-20; *Part Two* makes the case that this Glory is God the Son, the Messenger of Yahweh (see pp. 69-71).

Israel complained about the lack of food, and the *glory* of Yahweh appeared to declare His provision of manna and quail (16:7, 10). When Israel made it to Mount Sinai, Yahweh manifested His *glory* on the mountain in fire, thunders, lightnings, a loud trumpet blast, and trembling.[50] These encounters demonstrate God's desire for His people to see His glory, revere His awesome holiness and power, believe, and obey His commandments that they may worshipfully enjoy His covenant love.[51]

However, while Moses was on the mountain with God for forty days and nights, Israel broke the covenant by committing idolatry, exchanging the glory of God for an image of a golden calf (Ex. 32, Jer. 2:11, Rom. 1:23). God justly told Moses, "Now therefore let me alone, that my wrath may burn hot against them and I may consume them, in order that I may make a great nation of you" (32:10). *Moses interceded for Israel by appealing to God's reputation:* "Why should the Egyptians say, 'With evil intent did he bring them out, to kill them in the mountains and to consume them from the face of the earth'? Turn from your burning anger and relent from this disaster against your people" (32:12). God relented (32:14), and we gained an example that *our priority in prayer should be the glory of God.*[52]

God later added commentary to Israel's time in the wilderness through the prophet Ezekiel. First, God said of the Exodus:

> *"I acted for the sake of my name*, that it should not be profaned in the sight of the nations among whom they lived, in whose sight *I made myself known to them* in bringing them out of the land of Egypt" (Ezek. 20:9).

Then God said of Israel's sinfulness and His mercy in the wilderness:

---

50. Ex. 19:16-20, 24:16-17
51. Ex. 14:31; 19:9; 20:6, 20; 24:10-11
52. See also p. 77 on Mt. 6:9.

> "...Then I said I would pour out my wrath upon them in the wilderness, to make a full end of them. [14]But *I acted for the sake of my name*, that it should not be profaned in the sight of the nations..." (20:13-14).

Finally, God spoke of the second generation in the wilderness (20:18), which also could have been justly forbidden entrance to the Promised Land (20:21-22):

> "...Then I said I would pour out my wrath upon them and spend my anger against them in the wilderness. [22]But I withheld my hand and *acted for the sake of my name*, that it should not be profaned in the sight of the nations."

Thus God revealed three times His motive for merciful patience with Israel in the Exodus and wilderness: the glory of His Name.

Yahweh commanded Israel to build a tabernacle as a copy of His heavenly temple because He desires that His glory dwell on the earth (Ex. 25:8, Heb. 8:5). Nearly every material was to be overlaid with gold or precious stones to depict God's beauty, purity, and worth (e.g., Ex. 28:2 ff.). Yahweh said (in 29:43-46):

> There I will meet with the people of Israel, and it [tabernacle] shall be *sanctified by My glory*.... [45]I will dwell among the people of Israel and will be their God. [46]And they shall *know that I am Yahweh* their God, who brought them out of the land of Egypt that I might dwell among them. *I am Yahweh* their God.

After meticulous instructions for building this holy space, the book of Exodus ends with its completion:

> Then the cloud covered the tent of meeting, and the *glory* of Yahweh filled the tabernacle. [35]And Moses was not able to enter the tent of meeting because the cloud settled on it, and the *glory* of Yahweh filled the tabernacle (40:34-35).

This filling of the tabernacle foreshadowed that great day when God's glory will fill the whole earth.[53]

The book of Leviticus expounds on the commandments God graciously gave so that He would be propitiated[54] for Israel's sins and so "that the glory of Yahweh may appear to [them]" (9:6-7). The sacrifice of animals according to specific laws temporarily[55] appeased God's wrath for Israel's sins. If God's holiness was to "go public" among Israel, then she must believe and obey by seeking forgiveness according to God's will.

The book of Numbers resumes the Exodus narrative one month after the completion of the tabernacle. It chronicles how the glory of Yahweh repeatedly appeared to punish the disobedient (Num. 14:10; 16:19, 42; 20:6) with judgment for sin again defined in the context of those who had seen God's glory and signs and yet had disobeyed (14:22).

FOR THE SAKE OF GLORY IN THE PROMISED LAND

God brought Joshua and Israel into the Promised Land in the typological way He had taken Moses and Israel out of Egypt: miraculously through water (Josh. 3-4, esp. 4:23). God stopped the flow of the Jordan River at a city called Adam (3:16), so that He Himself[56] could lead Israel through on dry ground. The people were commanded to tell future generations God's motivation for the event: *"so that all the peoples of the earth may know that the hand of Yahweh is strong,* that you may revere Yahweh your God all the days"* (4:24, AT).

God defeated His enemies in order to give Israel the Promised Land for the glory of His Name, as evidenced in King David's prayer in 2 Samuel 7:22-24:

---

53. Num. 14:21, Isa. 11:9, Hab. 2:14, Ps. 72:19, Rev. 21:11, 22-23; see Beale, *The Temple and the Church's Mission.*

54. For God to be propitiated is to have His wrath appeased by substitution, in order that His righteous wrath may be turned into unmerited favor. See "A Celebration of Propitiation" (ProjectOne28.com/good-friday).

55. Heb. 10:1-4, Rom. 3:25

56. ESV footnotes the literal Hebrew of Joshua 3:11: "Behold, the ark of the covenant,

> Therefore you are great, O Yahweh, God. For there is none like you, and there is no God besides you, according to all that we have heard with our ears. And who is like your people Israel, the one nation on earth whom God went to redeem to be his people, *making himself a name* and doing for them great and awesome things by driving out before your people, whom you redeemed *for yourself* from Egypt, a nation and its gods? And you established *for yourself* your people Israel to be your people forever. And you, O Yahweh, became their God.

Indeed, Joshua, who led the conquests of the Promised Land, had prayed similarly for victory over Ai: "What will you do *for your great name?*" (Josh. 7:9).

In the time of Judges, God whittled down Gideon's army to a mere 300, "lest Israel boast over me" (7:2), so that He alone would gain glory through their miraculous victory (7:15, 22). When Eli's worthless sons were priests, blaspheming God, He enabled the Philistines to conquer Israel and steal the Ark.[57] Then it was said, "The glory has departed from Israel..." (1 Sam. 4:21-22). However, God could not allow the Philistines to gloat as though their god Dagon were greater than Yahweh, so He knocked over the idol, making it appear as though Dagon was bowing before Him on the Ark (5:1-3). The next night Yahweh knocked over and broke off the head and hands of Dagon (5:4). Just as Yahweh judged the gods of Egypt, He judged the Philistines' god. Also reminiscent of the Exodus, Yahweh's plagues (5:6-12) caused the Philistines to "give glory to the God of Israel" (6:5) and let the Ark go out of captivity.

Though Israel was sinful in the Promised Land, God spared them for the glory of His Name, according to the prophet Samuel:

> "Do not be afraid; you have done all this evil. Yet do not turn

---

the Lord of all the earth *is passing over* before you..." (emphasis mine). This brings out the faith statement that Yahweh Himself was seated on the ark, as King on His throne, while they crossed the river.

57. 1 Sam. 2:12-17; 3:13; 4:3, 10-11

aside from following Yahweh, but serve Yahweh with all your heart.… [22]For Yahweh will not forsake His people, *for His great Name's sake*, because it has pleased Yahweh to make you a people *for Himself*" (1 Sam. 12:20-22).

Like those at the Tower of Babel, King Saul showed more concern for his honor than God's (1 Sam. 15:12, 30), so he was rejected and judged. Saul was held up in contrast to David (15:28), who risked his life and *slayed Goliath out of jealousy for God's reputation* (1 Sam. 17:26, 36). Indeed, David confidently proclaimed to Goliath:

> I come to you in the name of Yahweh of armies, the God of Israel's ranks, whom you have defied. [46]This day Yahweh will deliver you into my hand… *that all the earth may know* that there is a God in Israel, [47]and that all this assembly *may know that Yahweh saves* not with sword or spear. Because the battle is Yahweh's… (17:45-47, AT).

As king, David's delight in God's messianic promise was that "your name will be magnified forever."[58] David knew God was leading him "in paths of righteousness for his name's sake."[59] He instituted unceasing worship to Yahweh around the Ark (on earth as it is in heaven),[60] organizing 4,000 Levites into shifts of singers and musicians.[61] David himself was first and foremost a worshiper, composing psalms and directing the people: "Glory in his holy name," "Declare His glory among the nations," "Ascribe to Yahweh glory and strength! *Ascribe to Yahweh the glory due his name!*"[62] David's last words in Chronicles, after praising God's "glorious name," instructed the nation: "Bless Yahweh your God."[63] David was a man according to God's own heart and

---

58. 2 Sam. 7:26, 1 Chron. 17:24

59. Ps. 23:3, cf. 31:3, 138:2, 5

60. Sam McVay, Jr., "1 Chronicles 15," 6 Feb 2011 (NewLifeEquip.com/resourcelibrary.cfm?id=8964).

61. 1 Chron. 16, 23, 25, esp. 23:5

62. Respectively, 1 Chron. 16:10, 16:24, 16:28-29

will.[64] Therefore, *we see God's purpose in David's purpose: the glory of the Name of Yahweh.*

Yahweh directed Solomon to build a house "for My Name," that is, for Himself and for His reputation[65] – a place to manifest His ownership and kingship as well as a place to receive worship. Solomon dedicated the temple (the permanent version of the portable tabernacle) with this prayer:

> Likewise, when a foreigner, who is not of your people Israel, comes from a far country *for your name's sake* [42](for they shall hear of *your great name* and your mighty hand, and of your outstretched arm), when he comes and prays toward this house, [43]hear in heaven your dwelling place and do according to all for which the foreigner calls to you, *in order that all the peoples of the earth may know your name* and fear you, as do your people Israel… (1 Ki. 8:41-43, cf. 8:60).

As with Moses' tabernacle, the glory of Yahweh filled Solomon's temple as a foreshadow of God's plans to fill all things with His glory.[66]

When Israel was ensnared in idolatry with the Canaanites' false god, Baal, the prophet Elijah was jealous for the glory of Yahweh. He set up a competition with the prophets of Baal to prove their god was not real, but Yahweh is. He prayed publicly (1 Ki. 18:36-39) that God would prove Himself by consuming his sacrifice:

> "O *Yahweh*, God of Abraham, Isaac, and Israel, let it be known this day that you are God in Israel, and that I am your servant, and that I have done all these things at your word. [37]Answer me, O *Yahweh*, answer me, *that this people*

---

63. Respectively, 1 Chron. 29:13 and 29:20.

64. Acts 13:22, 36; 1 Sam. 13:14

65. 2 Sam. 7:13; 1 Chr. 22:10; 1 Ki. 5:5. Hamilton, *God's Glory in Salvation through Judgment*, 172. Name Personified: Isa. 30:27.

66. Cf. p. 33 (and n. 53 on p. 34). 2 Chron. 5:13, 14; 7:1, 2, 3.

may know that you, O Yahweh, are God, and that you have
turned their hearts back." [38]Then the fire of Yahweh fell and
consumed the burnt offering…. [39]And when all the people
saw it, they fell on their faces and said, "*Yahweh*, he is God;
Yahweh, he is God!"

Clearly, this is the kind of prayer Yahweh delights to answer.

When Assyria's king mocked the living God and threatened
to destroy Jerusalem, *Hezekiah king of Judah interceded by
appealing to Yahweh's reputation in all the earth:* "Yahweh our
God, save us, please from his hand, that all the kingdoms of the
earth may *know that You, O Yahweh, are God alone.*"[67] The king
received God's response through the prophet Isaiah: Assyria's
king "shall not come into this city, declares Yahweh. For I will
defend this city to save it, *for my own sake* and for the sake of my
servant David" (19:33-34).[68]

In these Scriptures (and many more that could be cited,
such as the entire book of Psalms), we see that God's servants
share His jealousy for His fame and that God's greatest goal in
all of His works is the glory of His Name.

FOR THE SAKE OF GLORY IN THE EXILE

Though the nation of Israel was created to be God's glory,
praise, and Name (Jer. 13:11), they continually tarnished His
reputation by their unbelief and idolatry. If God did not act in
righteous judgment, then He would not be true to Himself, and
the nations would not know His glory (Isa. 26:8-11, below).

God prophesied as early as Moses, even before Israel
entered the Promised Land, that they would forsake Him, break
the covenant, and be punished with exile.[69] After Solomon's

---

67. 2 Ki. 19:19, cf. Isa. 37:20.

68. "For the sake of my servant David" implied God's concern for His faithfulness (part
of His glory, Ex. 34:6-7), upholding His messianic promise (e.g., 2 Sam. 7:11-16).

69. Dt. 4:25-31, 30:1-10, 31:16-32:47, cf. Isa. 48:8.

apostasy, the kingdom divided into the ten tribes of "Israel" in the north and "Judah" (which also encompassed Simeon) in the south. Each experienced a succession of mostly evil kings who led a mostly evil nation. Anticipating a northern invasion, *Joel called the people to repentance and prayer for the sake of God's reputation:* "Why should they say among the peoples, 'Where is their God?'" (2:17). The prophets repeatedly warned both Judah and Israel, but neither nation repented.[70]

God "whistled for" Assyria to defeat and deport the northern tribes and then empowered King Nebuchadnezzar of Babylon to destroy Jerusalem and carry off the southern tribes.[71] Israel was exiled for the "multitude of her transgressions" (Lam. 1:5), which could be summed up into one word: idolatry.[72] They were hypocrites, feigning worship of Yahweh while committing evil deeds and blatantly worshiping the false gods of the surrounding nations.[73] Yahweh, the God jealous for the goodness of His Name in saving and judging, would not let His people go unpunished (Am. 2:4–3:2) because they had "profaned [His] holy name" (2:7).

Six years into Judah's exile, before Jerusalem had been destroyed, God showed Ezekiel a vision of the "image of jealousy, which provokes to jealousy" (8:3, 5) – all of the idolatrous abominations the priests were doing for other gods *inside* the temple! "Because [they] have defiled my sanctuary…. I will vent my fury upon them and satisfy myself. And *they shall know that I am Yahweh* – that I have spoken in my jealousy" (5:11, 13). Seventy-two times God spoke through Ezekiel that people would *"know that I am Yahweh."* Seventy-two. God purposed the glory of His Name, not only through the exile, but also through

---

70. 2 Chron. 36:15-16, Jer. 44:4-5

71. Respectively, 2 Ki. 17:6; Isa. 5:26, 7:18 and 2 Chr. 36:17-21

72. Hos. 2:13; Zeph. 1:2-6; Jer. 1:16, 2:11, 2:28, 5:19, 16:10-13; Mic. 1:5; Ezek. 5:11; 2 Chr. 34:25

73. Isa. 1, 29:13; Jer. 5:28-29, 11:1-8; Mic. 3:8-12

His judgments upon the other nations and His restoration of His people.[74]

FOR THE SAKE OF GLORY
IN THE PROMISED RESTORATION

As early as the time when Moses prophesied the exile, he prophesied Israel's repentance and restoration (Dt. 4:27-31), and succeeding prophets did the same (e.g., Jer. 29:10-14). *One of the motivations for which God would judge the nations and restore Israel was His reputation:*

> I would have said, "I will cut them [Israel] to pieces;
> > I will wipe them from human memory,"
> [27]had I not feared provocation by the enemy,
> > lest their adversaries should misunderstand,
> lest they should say, "Our hand is triumphant,
> > it was not Yahweh who did all this" (Dt. 32:26-27).

Isaiah, after prophesying judgment on Israel, modeled anticipation for God to judge the nations, as well (26:8-11):

> In the path of your judgments,
> > O Yahweh, we wait for you;
> *Your name and remembrance*[75]
> > *are the desire of our soul.*
> [9]...For when your judgments are in the earth,
> > the inhabitants of the world learn righteousness.
> [10]If favor is shown to the wicked,
> > he does not learn righteousness;
> in the land of uprightness he deals corruptly
> > and does not *see the majesty of Yahweh.*
> [11]O Yahweh, your hand is lifted up,
> > but they do not see it.
> Let them *see your jealousy* for your people, and be ashamed.
> > Let the fire for your adversaries consume them.

---

74. The exile was because of jealousy (Deut. 29:20, 32:16, 21; 1 Ki. 14:22; Ezek. 5:13, 8:3, 8:5, 16:42, 23:25, 36:6, 38:19; Ps. 78:58-59), the judgment upon the nations was because of jealousy (Ezek. 36:5, Nah. 1:2, Zeph. 1:18, 3:8; Zech. 1:14, 8:2), and the restoration was because of jealousy (Ezek. 39:25, Joel 2:18).

Judgment against the wicked is part of the glory and goodness of God (Ex. 34:6-7), and His servants want the nations to see His majesty through judgment (praying, "in wrath, remember mercy," Hab. 3:2).

God used Assyria and Babylon to judge His people. However, because those nations were exceedingly wicked themselves, God brought judgment upon Assyria through Babylon and upon Babylon through Cyrus, king of Persia. God actually named Cyrus through Isaiah more than 150 years before he was born.[76] He called this pagan king His "anointed one" (*messiah*, "christ") because he was empowered by God to free a remnant of Israelites to return to Jerusalem, rebuild the temple, and resume worship (Isa. 45:1-13). Then all would know the exile was not because of Yahweh's weakness, but because of His justice in punishing Israel's sins.[77] God prophesied to Cyrus, "I equip you, though you do not know me, *⁶that people may know*, from the rising of the sun and from the west, *that there is none besides me; I am Yahweh*, and there is no other" (Isa. 45:5-6).

Isaiah prophesied that judgments would come upon Israel, but not as fully as they deserved[78] because of God's jealousy for His glory. The passage below, coming in the context of how and why God would rescue Israel from Babylon through Cyrus, illustrates this clearly:

> *"For my name's sake* I defer my anger,
>   *for the sake of my praise* I restrain it for you,
>   that I may not cut you off.
> ¹⁰Behold, I have refined you, but not as silver;
>   I have tried you in the furnace of affliction.
> ¹¹*For my own sake, for my own sake*, I do it,

---

75. See *Part Two*, p. 20, for the significance of "remembrance" and "name."

76. Isa. 44:28-45:13. Norman L. Geisler, *A Popular Survey of the Old Testament* (Grand Rapids, MI: BakerBooks, 2007), 247.

77. Cf. Ezek. 39:21-24.

78. Cf. Ezra 9:13.

> for how should *my name* be profaned?
> *My glory* I will not give to another (48:9-11, cf. 42:8).

No king of Assyria or Babylon – no other person at all – deserves the glory due only to the one true God. Therefore, God promised to conquer those captors so that a restored remnant would again "praise the Name of Yahweh" (Joel 2:26-27), and then "nations will bless themselves in Him, and in Him they will boast" (Jer. 4:2, AT).

God spoke strongly through Ezekiel that the new exodus, new covenant, and new creation would not come because of Israel's merit, but because of His jealousy for His holy Name to be known:

> *I had concern for my holy name....* [22]It is not for your sake, O house of Israel, that I am about to act, but *for the sake of my holy name*, which you have profaned among the nations to which you came. [23]And *I will vindicate the holiness of my great name*, which has been profaned among the nations, and which you have profaned among them. And *the nations will know that I am Yahweh*, declares the Lord Yahweh, when through you *I vindicate my holiness* before their eyes.[79]

Ezekiel had seen the Glory of God depart from the temple, and he also *saw the Glory of God return to an expanded temple that filled the land.*[80] Though Israel had failed, God would not fail in His mission to fill the earth with His glory through image-bearers filled with His Spirit.[81]

Daniel was exiled to Babylon where he rebuked the self-glorification of King Nebuchadnezzar and King Belshazzar.[82] Yet

---

79. Ezek. 36:21-23, cf. v. 32; see n. 7 on pp. 7-8 for the holiness/glory connection.

80. Ezek. 10:1-22 and 43:1-5. More on this Glory Personified in the next chapter. G. K. Beale makes a brilliant case that this temple is non-structural, and it has been inaugurated, but not yet consummated, in Christ and His Church (*The Temple and the Church's Mission*, 335-364).

81. Ezek. 36:22-37:14; cf. the note above about the human temple.

82. Dan. 4:19-37 and ch. 5

Daniel was preserved by God until the end of the seventy years (the prophesied length of the exile, Jer. 25:12, Dan. 9:2). He was one who fulfilled the prophecies of exilic confession, repentance, and prayer for restoration (Dan. 9:3-15), by interceding (9:17-19) on behalf Israel for the sake of God's Name:

> Now therefore, O our God, listen to the prayer of your servant and to his pleas for mercy, and *for your own sake*, O Lord, make your face to shine upon your sanctuary, which is desolate. O my God, incline your ear and hear. Open your eyes and see our desolations, and *the city that is called by your name*. For we do not present our pleas before you because of our righteousness, but *because of your great mercy.* O Lord, hear; O Lord, forgive. O Lord, pay attention and act. Delay not, *for your own sake, O my God, because your city and your people are called by your name.*

God honored Daniel's Name-centered prayer with angelic and divine visitations,[83] revelations of the future, and Israel's restoration.

God *began* to fulfill His promises when Cyrus conquered Babylon, permitted the Jewish exiles to return home, and funded the rebuilding of the temple in Jerusalem.[84] The temple was rededicated and sacrifices resumed, but God's glory was not reported to have filled this temple as it did for Moses and Solomon.[85] Ezra and Nehemiah both lamented that the people of Israel were still slaves (now to Persia) and still sinful.[86] They experienced no kingly Messiah, no new covenant, no outpouring of the Spirit, no resurrection, no greater temple, no ingathering of the nations, and no new creation.[87]

---

83. See *Part Two*, pp. 75-79, on the mysterious (divine?) figure of Daniel 10.

84. 2 Chr. 36:22-23, Ezra 1

85. Cf. Ezra 3:12, Hag. 2:3. An argument from silence – but after Ezekiel 43:1-5, it is a deafening silence. Yet it is not truly silence, considering that Malachi 3:1-2 (eighty years later!) makes clear that Yahweh still had not returned to the temple. See "Tying the Two Testaments Together: Part Two" (ProjectOne28.com/testaments).

86. Ezr. 9:9, Neh. 9:36. J. G. McConville, "Ezra-Nehemiah and the Fulfillment of

HOPE OF GLORY

The Old Testament thus closed with God's people still waiting for the messianic King and Servant who would accomplish all God had promised. This history demonstrated that God did everything for His glory – the supreme worth above all things – and promised to do even more for His glory. Tellingly, the last prophet in the Old Testament, Malachi, relayed Yahweh's rebuke to priests who despised His Name (1:6):

> For from the rising of the sun to its setting *My Name will be great among the nations*, and in every place incense will be offered *to My Name*, and a pure offering. For *My Name will be great among the nations*, says Yahweh of armies. [14]...For I am a great King, says Yahweh of armies, and *My Name will be revered among the nations* (1:11, 14, AT).

The hope of a repentant Israelite could not lie in himself or his leaders, but only in Yahweh's relentless commitment to His glory.[88]

When we turn to the New Testament, we find unveiled what was a secret in the Old: the Glory of God is more than a mere manifestation or an abstract ideal; the Glory of God is a Person.

Prophecy," *Vetus Testamentum*, Vol. 36, Fasc. 2 (Apr., 1986), pp. 205-224.

87. More in "HIStory: Session 7, The Exile and the Prophetic Promises" (ProjectOne28. com/HIStory).

88. For example, Malachi 3:6, "For I, Yahweh, do not change; *therefore* you, O children of Jacob, are not consumed."

CHAPTER TWO

GLORY IS A PERSON

In the beginning, God purposed creation for His glory, yet that creation was devastated when Satan and the rebellious one-third of the angels were cast down to the earth.[1] God created Man to subdue the enemy and fill the earth with the image of His glory. Man, however, joined the rebellion. Still, God prophesied the serpent would be crushed by a Seed of Eve – an Anointed One and His people.[2] "In that day," Isaiah foretold, "the Branch of Yahweh" – a Name for this Anointed Seed – "will be beautiful and glorious."[3] God had formed an astounding plan before the foundation of the world,[4] and when the fullness of time came (Gal. 4:4), He appeared.

THE ETERNAL SON, THE GLORY OF GOD

The Spirit wrote through the apostle John that a Name for God's Son is the Word. As the Word, He is the Self-expression of

---

1. *Light Shines in the Darkness: Scriptures Interpreting the Spiritual Drama of Genesis 1:2-3* (El Dorado, KS: Project one28 Publishing, 2010), free at ProjectOne28.com.

2. Genesis 3:15. "Seed" is a collective singular in Hebrew, referring here to One Man and the one group in Him (cf. Rom. 16:20). See James Hamilton, "The

God the Father. Because the Father is eternal, the Word is eternal
– God without cause and with the Father from the beginning
(1:1-4).[5] "And the Word became flesh and tabernacled among
us, and we beheld His glory – glory as of the One-of-a-kind[6]
Son, from the Father, full of grace and truth" (1:14, AT). In the
Old Testament, the glory of God would dwell in the tabernacle
of Moses or the temple of Solomon; but circa 4 B.C.[7] *the glory of
God came down and tabernacled in a Man named Jesus*, conceived
of the Holy Spirit through a virgin.[8]

Given the New Exodus context, when John wrote that the
Word made flesh was "full of grace and truth" (or "truthfulness"),
this was probably his own rendering of the Hebrew in Yahweh's
definition of His glory in Exodus 34:6-7,[9] which the ESV
translates "steadfast love and faithfulness." In other words, Jesus
is full of what God is. To behold Jesus is to behold the glory of
Yahweh – if one has eyes to see it. Therefore, Jesus could say to
His disciples, "The one, having seen *Me* has seen the Father" (Jn.
14:9, AT).

The beloved Son "is the image of the unseen God…. in Him
all the fullness of Godhood is dwelling bodily."[10] "Dwelling" is
also temple language; God was said to "dwell" in His temple (e.g.,

---

Skull Crushing Seed of the Woman: Inner-Biblical Interpretation of Genesis
3:15," *SBJT* 10:2 (Summer 2006), 30-54 (free at jimhamilton.info/wp-content/
uploads/2008/04/hamilton_sbjt_10-2.pdf).

3.   Isa. 4:2, cf. Isa. 11:1; Jer. 23:5, 33:15; Zech. 3:8, 6:12

4.   1 Pet. 1:2, 1:20; Eph. 1:4; 2 Tim. 1:9; Mt. 13:35, 25:34; Rev. 13:8, 17:8

5.   See *Part Two*, 117-120, for more on John 1:1-4.

6.   Translators in the past thought the Greek compound *monogenēs* owed its meaning
to *mono* (only) plus *genaō* (to beget), thus rendering "only begotten Son" (KJV).
But this is incorrect. *Monogenēs* comes from *mono* and *genos* (genus, kind).
"Begotten" suggests made, caused to exist, but Jesus is eternal and uncaused.
Scripture emphasizes He is the Father's "One-of-a-kind." We find confirmation in
Hebrews 11:17, which calls Isaac the *monogenēs* of Abraham, who in fact had six
other sons: his firstborn Ishmael (Gen. 16:15) and five from Keturah (25:1-2). Isaac
was not the only begotten, but he was one-of-a-kind – the only son from God's
promise of a miracle in Sarah's old, barren womb (Gen. 17:15-21). See, e.g., D. A.
Carson, *Exegetical Fallacies*, Second Edition (Grand Rapids, MI: Baker Academic,

Mt. 23:21). When Jesus came, God dwelled not in the physical temple of Herod, but in the body of Jesus. Therefore, Jesus said, "Something greater than the temple is here" (Mt. 12:6), and, "'Destroy this temple, and in three days I will raise it up.' ...he was speaking about the temple of his body" (Jn. 2:19, 21). The body of Jesus houses the glorious presence of God because He is the God-Man, God the Son in flesh. His body/temple would be destroyed on the Cross, but rebuilt at the resurrection!

Hebrews 1:3 says God's Son is "the radiance of His glory and the exact representation of His Being, and carrying all things by the word of His power…" (AT).[11] We noted in the Introduction that glory is one's nature made manifest. God's Being is so perfect and infinite that it does not manifest only as an idea or a reputation or a light; God's Being eternally manifests as a perfect, full, infinite Person: His Son. *The radiant Glory of God is the Son of God.*

This truth ought to affect all of our thoughts about God's glory – and everything else. Michael Reeves says well that "the Trinity is the governing center of all Christian belief, the truth that shapes and beautifies all others."[12] The manifestation of God through the Son tells us so much about His nature. Reeves adds,

---

1996), 30-31; Andreas J. Köstenberger, *John*, BECNT (Grand Rapids, MI: Baker Academic, 2004), 42-44, 49 (and the literature in his notes 72-75). But, for the recent work of Lee Irons and Denny Burk calling for reevaluation of this word and the doctrine of the Son's "eternal generation," see ProjectOne28.com/begotten.

7. Dr. Floyd Nolen Jones, *The Chronology of the Old Testament*, 16th Edition (Green Forest, AR: MasterBooks, 1993-2004), 205-254 (also cited on pages 3-4 of ProjectOne28.com/Daniels_Seventy_Weeks.pdf).

8. Mt. 1:18-25, Lk. 1:26-38

9. George Eldon Ladd, *A Theology of the New Testament*, Revised Edition, ed. Donald A. Hagner (Grand Rapids: Eerdmans, 1993), 266; D. A. Carson, *The Gospel according to John*, PNTC (Grand Rapids, MI: Eerdmans, 1991), 129.

10. Col. 1:15… 2:9, AT (cf. 1:19; 2 Cor. 4:4).

11. See *Part Two*, 138-139, for more on Heb. 1:3.

12. *Delighting in the Trinity: An Introduction to the Christian Faith* (Downers Grove, IL: InterVarsity Press, 2012), 16. I wish everyone would read this delightful book.

> The God [whom the Son] reveals is, first and foremost, a
> Father.... Before he ever created, before he ever ruled the
> world, before anything else, this God was a Father loving
> his Son.... Since God is, before all things, a Father, and not
> primarily a Creator or Ruler, all his ways are beautifully
> fatherly... all that he does he does as a Father.[13]

When we speak of the glory of God, we mean the
manifestation of the Triune God. Before the founding of the
world, when all that existed was God, He was not lonely. For
eternity past the Father has been loving and delighting in the
Son and Spirit, the Son in the Father and Spirit, and the Spirit
in the Father and Son – a raging, uncontainable, joyfest of love.
The Father, who eternally gives life, love, and joy to His Son
through the Spirit, is fundamentally a generous, life-generating,
glory-giving, joy-sharing kind of God. Therefore, we cannot
entertain the thought for a moment that this Triune God created
out of lack or some sense of need. Rather, He created out of the
abundance of joy in His Glory that He may share His joy in His
Glory – in other words, that He may share His joy in His *Son*.

For this reason, the baptism of Jesus truly does peel back
the curtain of the heavens for us to glimpse the essence of the
Trinity. The Son is center stage, loving His Father in joyful
obedience.[14] The Father rips heaven open to shout His approval:
"This is My beloved Son, in whom I am delighted!"[15] And the
Father communicates His love and delight by bestowing His
Spirit upon His incarnate Son without measure.[16]

In this we begin to see the eternal purpose of God. Elsewhere
I might simply define the purpose for all things as "the glory of
God in the preeminence of Christ." Here I register the fuller
meaning inherent in that kind of Biblical shorthand: God the

---

13. *Ibid.*, 21, 23. See especially Jn. 17:24-26.

14. Jesus baptism is recounted in Mt. 3:13-17. For Jesus' loving, joyful obedience, see
    vv. 13-15 and cf. Jn. 14:31, Ps. 40:8 (applied to Jesus in Heb. 10:5-7), and Heb.
    12:2. I am grateful to God that Michael Reeves freshly awakened my appreciation
    for this event in his book *Delighting in the Trinity*, 29.

Father wants His image-bearers to share His delight in His glorious Son by putting that love and delight for His Son in us by His Spirit.[17] This is the glorious gospel that we will unpack in the remainder of the book.

THE SON AS GOD'S GLORY BEFORE THE INCARNATION

The Old Testament contains in secret what the New Testament unveils in plain language: the Son of God was the radiant Glory of God even before becoming flesh and receiving the human Name "Jesus." *Part Two* will thoroughly illustrate this, but here we will focus on one passage that especially pertains to our specific topic of *glory*.

The exiled Ezekiel saw a vision of God's heavenly temple (of which the temple in Jerusalem was only a shadow, Heb. 8:1-5). His record of the vision illustrates the struggle for earthly language to describe such un-earthly realities, saying something was "like" this or "like the appearance of" that, but clearly something better and beyond this or that. In the midst of fascinating surroundings, Ezekiel 1:26-28:

> …there was the likeness of a throne, in appearance like sapphire; and *seated above the likeness of a throne was a likeness with a human appearance*. And upward from what had the appearance of his waist I saw as it were gleaming metal, like the appearance of fire enclosed all around. And downward from what had the appearance of his waist I saw as it were the appearance of fire, and there was brightness around him. Like the appearance of the bow that is in the cloud on the day of rain, so was the appearance of the brightness all around. Such was *the appearance of the likeness of the glory of Yahweh*. And when I saw it, I fell on my face, and I heard the voice of one speaking.

---

15. Mt. 3:17. This truth is so precious (and so essential that we share the Father's heart in it) that the Spirit led Matthew to give it to us twice more: 12:18 and 17:5.

16. Mt. 3:16 with Jn. 3:34-35 and Rom. 5:5

17. See esp. Jn 17:24-26 with 8:42, and also Reeves, 43-44, 69, 76, 87, 94-95.

Even before the Incarnation, the Glory of Yahweh on His throne manifested *like* a human appearance. He was not human, but He appeared *like* a human – because we are like Him (Gen. 1:26). God does not have flesh and bones; He is spirit.[18] Yet we look like we do and manifest like we do because we are in the likeness of the Glory of Yahweh.

Later in Ezekiel's experience, he recounted, "And the hand of Yahweh was upon me there. And he said to me, 'Arise, go out into the valley, and there I will speak with you'" (3:22). Note that the promise was that *Yahweh* would speak with him.

> "So I arose and went out into the valley, and behold, *the Glory of Yahweh stood there*, like the Glory whom I had seen by the Chebar canal [1:26-28, qtd. above], and I fell on my face. [24]But the Spirit entered into me and set me on my feet, and *He spoke with me...*" (3:23-24, AT).

The Glory stood! The Glory spoke! Glory is not a thing, but a Person. The Glory of Yahweh is Yahweh Himself, the Son (cf. Heb. 1:3). In fact, John 12:41 explains that when Isaiah saw the King, Yahweh of armies, high and lifted up on His throne (Isa. 6:1-5), what Isaiah actually saw was the glory of the pre-incarnate Jesus! *The radiant Glory of God is the Son of God.* And He became flesh to bring glory to God in all the earth.

FOR THE SAKE OF GLORY IN THE INCARNATION

We could give many reasons that God became flesh. He came to fulfill the Scriptures, to undo the works of the devil, to bear witness to the truth, to preach the gospel of the kingdom, to call sinners to repentance, to seek and save the lost, to serve and give His life as a ransom, to take away sins, and to save sinners.[19] All of these are wondrously true, but we should not make ourselves the primary focus. *The ultimate goal of the Incarnation*

---

18. Jn. 4:24; Lk. 24:39

19. Respectively, Mt. 5:17; 1 Jn. 3:8; Jn. 18:37; Mk. 1:38-39 and Isa. 61:1; Lk. 5:32; Lk. 19:10; Mk. 10:45; 1 Jn. 3:5; 1 Tim. 1:15

is the glory of God. Philippians 2, quoted in the Preface, celebrates the voluntary humbling of the Son to take the form of a human Servant (i.e., incarnation, 2:6-7), and Paul culminates this purpose with, "to the glory of God the Father!" (2:11).

I used to read that passage as though the Son did something contrary to His Godhood when He humbled Himself to become a Man. But then Gary Weins[20] taught me that God is humble, as He said through Isaiah:

> For thus says the One who is high and lifted up,
>   who inhabits eternity, whose name is Holy:
> *"I dwell* in the high and holy place,
>   and also *with him who is* of a contrite and *lowly* spirit,
> to revive the spirit of the lowly,
>   and to revive the heart of the contrite" (57:15).

Therefore, the Son glorified the humble God by becoming a lowly Man (Mt. 11:29) in order to dwell with the lowly. The angels recognized this purpose and responded accordingly: at the news of Jesus' birth, "suddenly there came with the angel a multitude of the army of heaven, praising God and saying, 'Glory to God in the highest!'" (Lk. 2:13-14, AT). After the shepherds visited Baby Jesus, they "returned, glorifying and praising God for all they had heard and seen" (2:20).

In Romans 15:8-9, Paul wrote of subordinate means unto the ultimate end, saying Christ became flesh for the glory of God among the nations:

> For I am saying Christ has become a servant of the circumcised for the sake of the truthfulness of God, in

---

20. I believe I heard this in more than one recording, possibly first in "The Father of Humility" from his *Come to Papa* series (burningheartministries.com/Store/Products/1000011436/BHM_Store_products/MP3_Downloads/Come_to_Papa.aspx). Also, Andrew Murray wrote, "Christ is the humility of God embodied in human nature…. As the love and condescension of God makes Him the benefactor and helper and servant of all, so Jesus of necessity was the Incarnate Humility" (*Humility: The Beauty of Holiness* [New York: Anson D. F. Randolph & Co.], 27-28, free at manybooks.net/titles/murrayaother08Humility.html).

order to confirm the promises ‚to‚ the forefathers, and ‚for‚ the nations *to glorify God* for mercy…" (AT).

The *ESV Study Bible* rightfully notes from this passage: "the worship of God is his ultimate aim in salvation history."[21]

FOR THE SAKE OF GLORY IN THE MINISTRY OF JESUS

The apostle John recorded Jesus' first sign as changing the water to wine, which He "did at Cana in Galilee, and manifested his glory" (Jn. 2:11). That is to say, Jesus manifested His glory (His radiant Being) as the One in whom the "Father of glory" dwelled (Eph. 1:17). Jesus never took sole credit for His miracles (Jn. 5:19 ff.), but He said His words and works bore witness to the reality that the Father dwelled in Him and did *His* works through Jesus (14:10-11). Jesus said, "I do not seek my own glory; there is One who seeks it, and he is the judge" (8:50). He said His Father is seeking glory. He is seeking glory from true worshipers (4:23) because He is worthy. Jesus also said, "The one who speaks on his own authority seeks his own glory; but the one who seeks the glory of him who sent him is true, and in him there is no falsehood" (Jn. 7:18, cf. 8:54, Heb. 5:5). *Jesus sought the glory of God the Father in everything He did.* That is what made Him sinless, faithful, and true.

Jesus performed miracles for the glory of God. Richard Melick, Jr., writes:

> Miracles bring the glory of God into the human sphere. God's glory has power to change circumstances, correcting evil and evidencing heaven's completeness. Miracles do not simply point people to God; they bring God to people, allowing them to receive and acknowledge His glory.[22]

---

21. 2182. Moo notes: "Paul's pairing of ἔλεος [*eleos*, "mercy"] and ἀλήθεια [*alētheia*, "truth" or "truthfulness"] in parallel preposition phrases may evoke the familiar OT combination of God's 'truth [or faithfulness] and mercy," as in Exodus 34:6-7 (*Romans*, 878, n. 32). Though John used χάρις (*charis*, "grace") in John 1:14, 17, ἔλεος [*eleos*, "mercy"] is the most common LXX rendering for the Hb. *ḥeseḏ* (which ESV commonly translates "steadfast love").

Repeatedly, both the ones who were healed and the rest who witnessed the healings glorified God because of Jesus' merciful power.[23] Matthew 15:31 summarizes: "So the crowd *marveled* as they saw the mute speaking, the crippled restored, and the lame walking, and the blind seeing; and *they glorified the God of Israel*" (NASB, cf. Jn. 5:20).[24]

Jesus' reaction to the ten lepers reveals His goal (God's glory)in healings. Ten lepers had asked for mercy, and Jesus commanded them:

> "Go and show yourselves to the priests." And as they went they were cleansed. Then one of them, when he saw that he was healed, turned back, *praising God with a loud voice;* and he fell on his face at Jesus' feet, *giving him thanks*. Now he was a Samaritan. Then Jesus answered, "Were not ten cleansed? Where are the nine? Was no one found to return and *give praise to God* except this foreigner?" And he said to him, "Rise and go your way; your faith has [saved you]" (Lk. 17:14-19).

Jesus raised Lazarus from the dead for the glory of God. When Jesus heard that His beloved friend was sick, He responded: "This illness does not lead to death. *It is for the glory of God, so that the Son of God may be glorified through it"* (Jn. 11:4, cf. 9:3). But in seeming contradiction, Jesus delayed two days, so that Lazarus died.[25] Jesus was then able to teach and prove, "I AM the resurrection and the life" (11:25, AT), saying to Lazarus' sister, "I told you that, *if you believe, you will see the glory of God*, did I not?" (11:40, AT). So many in the region believed in Jesus because of this manifestation of glory that "from that day on, [the Jewish leaders, 11:47] made plans to put him to death" (11:53) – and Lazarus, too (12:9-11).

---

22. *Op. cit.*, 92.

23. E.g., Mt. 9:8, 15:31; Mk. 2:12; Lk. 2:20, 5:25-26, 7:16, 13:13, 17:15, 18:43

24. Specifying that they praised the God "of Israel" hints that these were Gentiles in a Gentile region (cf. Rom. 3:29), which reminds us of the purpose in Romans 15:8-9.

25. 11:6, though Jesus considered it "sleep" from which to be awakened, 11:11. See *Part Two*, 54-55, for more on this passage and how "Jesus was loving" them in His delay.

For the Sake of Glory in the Death of Jesus

In Greek, the word "hour," as their smallest unit of time, could signify a "moment." In John 7:30, 8:20, and 16:32, Jesus' "hour" means specifically the event of His crucifixion.[26] John 12:23 also speaks specifically of Jesus' death, when He said, "The hour has come for the Son of Man to be glorified." This is made clear by Jesus' following statement: "Amen, amen, I am saying to you, unless the grain of wheat, having fallen to the ground, dies, it abides alone. But if it dies, it bears much fruit" (12:24, AT). He moved from "the hour... glorified" to "dies." Not only this, He soon said, "Now is my soul troubled. And what shall I say? 'Father, save me from this hour?'" (12:27). Jesus was troubled by the impending crucifixion. Therfore, the context confirms our assertion of 12:23: *the crucifixion was the hour in which Jesus was glorified, the hour in which His true nature was manifested.*[27] And there is more here.

The crucifixion of Jesus also glorified the Father. After Jesus asked His rhetorical question ("And what should I say, 'Father, save me from this hour'?"), Jesus declared His goal in enduring the Cross:

> "But I came to this hour on account of this: *'Father, glorify Your Name!'"* Then a voice came out of heaven: "I both glorified it and will glorify it again" (12:27-28, AT).

This passage, perhaps even more clearly than all the previous Scriptures, corrects thoughts that place the salvation of Man at the apex of God's plan. We often have framed the gospel as if

---

26. In *The Gospel according to John* as a whole, Jesus' "hour" was the interdependent events of His crucifixion, resurrection, and exaltation. In 13:1, "Jesus knew that his hour had come to depart out of this world to the Father." The ascension is the main event in view here, but before He ascended, He had to die and be raised. All three aspects must be considered together. Likewise, 7:39 reasons that "as yet the Spirit had not been given, because Jesus was not yet glorified." The Spirit was not given until Jesus ascended and sat on His Father's throne to receive and pour out the Holy Spirit to His disciples (cf. Acts 2:33). But again, Jesus could not be glorified in heaven, nor believers sealed with the Spirit, until He obeyed the Father's will that He die for sins and be raised. All three aspects must be considered together. For

Man was the ultimate goal: "Christ died for *you*, so *you* could go to heaven." (This is true, but not the fullness of truth. More on this below.) The prevalence of such humanistic thinking in the American church was evident in the popularity of the song, "Above All,"[28] which exchanged the glory of God for "me":

> You took the fall
> And thought of me, above all.

That is a sad distortion. In truth, Jesus thought "above all" about the glory of His Father, which is clear in John 12:27-28 and all of the Scriptures quoted in this book. *The ultimate reason Jesus died on the Cross was to glorify the Name of Yahweh*. Immediately after Jesus' purpose statement, the Father spoke from heaven that He would indeed glorify Himself on the Cross (12:28). Taking this with 12:23, James Hamilton comments, "Jesus and the Father are joined together to glorify one another at the Cross."[29]

Let us remember that to glorify means to manifest one's being. God had defined His glory in Exodus 34:6-7 (AT):

> "Yahweh, Yahweh, a God merciful and gracious, slow to anger, and abounding in steadfast love and faithfulness, keeping steadfast love for thousands, *bearing[30] iniquity and transgression and sin*, but who will by no means clear the guilty, visiting the iniquity of the fathers on the children and the children's children, to the third and the fourth generation."

The fullness of God's glory is both loving and judging, and *we most clearly see the glory of God on the Cross*. Jesus' voluntary death manifested God as the Holy One whose mercy and love

---

glorification as crucifixion, which led to exaltation, see also John 13:31-32 ("Now" is significant because Judas had just left to betray Christ to murderers) and 17:1-2, 4-6, 24 (and those in the main text above).

27. See below on Exodus 34:6-7, as well as *Part Two*, 111-113, on John 8:28 (lit.).

28. Written by Paul Joseph Baloche and Lenny Leblanc (Universal Music), popularized by Michael W. Smith.

29. Hamilton, *God's Glory in Salvation through Judgment*, 414.

30. See n. 16 on p. 10.

moved Him *to bear* His wrath against sinners *in Himself.* Before the Cross, God's righteousness was in question "because in his divine forbearance he had passed over former sins" without judging them as they deserved (Rom. 3:25). God put forward Christ Jesus as a wrath-absorbing, substitutionary sacrifice (3:25)[31] *"to demonstrate His righteousness* at the present time, so that He would be righteous and declare righteous the one who has faith in Jesus" (3:26 HCSB). Jesus' self-sacrifice shone forth the righteousness, wrath, love,[32] and mercy of God – His glory. Oh, for a sight fuller than Moses glimpsed, let us bow our heads to the earth and worship!

Jesus had said, "I have come in my Father's name" (Jn. 5:43). This is true literally and metaphorically. His Hebrew Name, *Yeshua*, means *Yahweh saves.*[33] And Jesus also came in the essential *character* of His Father. At the end of His ministry, resolved to endure the Cross, He was able to pray:

> "Father, the hour has come; *glorify your Son that the Son may glorify you.... I glorified you* on earth, having accomplished the work that you gave me to do. And now, Father, *glorify me* in your own presence with the *glory that I had with you before the world existed....* I have *manifested your name* to the people whom you gave me out of the world.... The glory that you have given me I have given to them.... I *made known to them your name*, and I will continue to make it known" (Jn. 17:1, 4-5, 6, 22, 26).

What an intimate glimpse into the Son's passionate priority for His Father's glory! Through condescending to our form, teaching truth, subduing the enemy, working miracles of mercy – and especially through His propitious death and resurrection – Jesus gave us the right representation of Yahweh, the manifestation of who God is. Jesus perfectly achieved His ultimate purpose: the glory of God.

---

31. See "A Celebration of Propitiation" at ProjectOne28.com/good-friday.

32. E.g., Rom. 5:8; 1 Jn. 3:16, 4:10

GLORY IN THE RESURRECTION,
ASCENSION, AND EXALTATION OF CHRIST

On the Cross, Jesus showed us the glory of the God who is holy and just and must release His wrath to punish sin – and who is so loving and merciful that He Himself would become the God-Man to absorb that wrath in Himself. The Father then raised Jesus back to life to show Himself as the God who is victorious over every enemy, even death, the God who *is* resurrection and life.[34]

"Christ was raised from the dead *by the glory* of the Father" (Rom. 6:4). His body was "raised in glory" (1 Cor. 15:43), and God "gave him glory" (1 Pet. 1:21). His resurrected body was saturated with the "Spirit of glory" (1 Pet. 4:14), so that His is the firstfruits of a "spiritual body" (1 Cor. 15:44), a "body of glory" (Phil. 3:21, AT).

Before His death, the transfiguration in front of Peter, James, and John had hinted at this resurrection glory, which was truly a return to His preexistent glory which He possessed all along, though veiled to the unbelieving.[35] "And he was transfigured before them, and his face *shone* like the sun, and his clothes became white as *light*" (Mt. 17:2, see Rev. 1:16, qtd. below). Then those disciples "saw his *glory*" (Lk. 9:32), and Peter later testified, "...we were eyewitnesses of his majesty. For... he received honor and glory from God the Father, and the voice was borne to him by the Majestic Glory, 'This is my beloved Son, with whom I am well pleased'" (2 Pet. 1:16-17, cf. Mt. 17:5). The Father – who is named *the Majestic Glory* – let the three disciples see something of the glory that He would again unveil through the Son when He was "taken up in glory" (1 Tim. 3:16) and seated at the right hand of Majesty (Heb. 1:3). A glory that delights the Father. A delight that He desires to share with us.

---

33. *NIDNTT*, 2:331. See *Part Two*, 60, 70 (also n. 22). Cf. Mt. 1:21.

34. Jn. 1:4; 5:21, 25-29; 11:25-27

Jesus had prayed that we would see His eternal glory: "Father,
I desire that they also, whom you have given me, may be with
me where I am, to see my glory that you have given me because
you loved me before the foundation of the world" (Jn. 17:24, cf.
17:5). In a preliminary answer to this prayer, John was granted
a vision of the enthroned, resurrected God-Man in Revelation
1:13-18 (AT):

> ... like ˌaˌ son ˌofˌ man, having been clothed in ˌaˌ long robe and
> having been wrapped at the chest with ˌaˌ golden sash. ¹⁴And
> His head and its hairs ˌwereˌ white like wool, white like snow,
> and His eyes like ˌaˌ flame of fire, ¹⁵and His feet like burnished
> bronze, as having been fired in ˌaˌ furnace, and His voice like
> the voice ˌofˌ many waters, ¹⁶and having in His right ˌhandˌ
> seven stars and coming out of His mouth ˌaˌ sharp double-
> edged sword, and His face is shining like the sun in its power.
> ¹⁷And when I saw Him, I fell at His feet like ˌaˌ dead ˌmanˌ, and
> He put His hand on me, saying, "Do not be fearing. I AM the
> first and the last ¹⁸and the Living ˌOneˌ, and I was dead, and
> behold, I am living into the ages ˌofˌ the ages, and I am having
> the keys ˌofˌ Death and Hades.

What a glorious God-Man! The First and the Last – the
image of the Alpha and the Omega (Rev. 22:13, 16; 1:8). "The
Lord of glory" crucified (1 Cor. 2:8) but alive forevermore!
We recognize this description of this fiery image of God from
the experience of Ezekiel when he saw the Glory seated on the
throne and then standing by the canal in Babylon.³⁶ Ezekiel truly
saw the glory that the Son possessed before the world existed
(Jn. 17:5, 24). The Son then humbled Himself to become an
obedient sacrifice, and therefore, God exalted Him (Phil. 2:6-
11) back into His eternal glory (Rev. 1).

Later, John saw a vision of Jesus as a Lamb having been
slain, yet He conquered (Rev. 5:5-6). Even Jesus' resurrected

---

35. Clear from verses like Jn. 17:5, 24; 1:14; 2:11.

36. 1:26-28, 3:23, qtd. on pp. 49-50. The description of Christ in Revelation 1 comes
    mostly from Daniel 7 and 10 – for teaching on the Godhood of Jesus in Daniel and

body boasts the scars of His Cross[37] to eternally display the glory of the God who bore His judgment to save those He loved. John saw the God-Man's glory, and we will see it at His second coming, when He appears in glory.[38]

It has been marvellously, joyfully clear – has it not? – that Jesus *did* everything for God's glory because He Himself *is* the radiant Glory of God. The next two chapters will unpack the implications for us, who have been saved *to do* everything for God's glory in Christ because we ourselves are being transformed *to be* God's glory in Christ.

Revelation, see *Part Two*, 141-148.

37. Jn. 20:25, 27-28

38. E.g., Mt. 16:27, 25:31; Titus 2:13; taught on p. 85 and *Part Two*, 125-126.

CHAPTER THREE

SAVED FOR GLORY

God saved us for the same reason that He does everything: Himself! We have already seen the promises of the new covenant motivated by jealousy to show His Name holy. He also said explicitly:

> "I, I am he
>> who blots out your transgressions *for my own sake,*
>> and I will not remember your sins" (Isa. 43:25).

We are not the main reason that God forgives us. He forgives us to be Himself – to show His glory and to recover His plan for us as glorifiers (e.g., Isa. 60:21, 61:3). God saved us to get us back to the blessed commission of Genesis 1:28 (cf. 12:3, Gal. 3:8-16). Salvation is not the end. *Salvation is the means to the end, which is the Glory of God indwelling image-bearers and filling all things – to the praise of the glory of His grace* (Eph. 1:6). Romans 15:7 says *Jesus welcomed us for the glory of God.* In Acts 15:14, James celebrated "how God first visited the Gentiles, to take from them a people *for his name."* First John 2:12 teaches unambiguously: "your sins have been forgiven *for the sake of His Name"* (AT).

Therefore, a truly repentant person desires forgiveness for more than his own preservation. David prayed, *"For the sake of Your Name*, Yahweh, forgive my iniquity, because it is abundant" (Ps. 25:11, AT, cf. 109:21). Asaph followed suit: "Help us, God of our salvation, *because of the glory of Your Name;* deliver us, and make propitiation on account of our sins, *for the sake of Your Name!"* (79:9, AT). Jeremiah prayed, "Though our iniquities testify against us, Yahweh, act *for the sake of Your Name....* Do not spurn us, *for the sake of Your Name"* (14:7, 21, AT).

In light of these truths, many gospel invitations in our day are placed in the wrong context: how to get to heaven, rather than how to become the glory God deserves and demands. Paris Reidhead delivered a sermon, which I highly recommend, entitled "Ten Shekels and a Shirt."[1] In it, he described the pragmatism and humanism that has crept into the church. He summed up a typical gospel invitation as, "Accept Jesus, so you can go to heaven! You don't want to go to that old, filthy, nasty, burning hell when there is a beautiful heaven up there! Now come to Jesus, so you can go to heaven!" And he called it an appeal to selfishness. He continued:

> ...this philosophical postulate, that the end of all being is the happiness of Man, has been sort of covered over with evangelical terms and biblical doctrine until God reigns in heaven for the happiness of Man, Jesus Christ was incarnate for the happiness of Man, all the angels exist in the host – everything is for the happiness of Man! And I submit to you that this is un-Christian! Isn't Man happy? Didn't God intend to make Man happy? Yes, but as a by-product and not a prime-product!

---

1. ParisReidheadBibleTeachingMinistries.org/Ten_Shekels_and_A_Shirt.html hosts the text and backstory; SermonIndex.net/modules/mydownloads/singlefile. php?lid=282, the audio.

…Let me summarize: Christianity says, "The end of all being is the glory of God." Humanism says, "The end of all being is the happiness of Man." And one was born in Hell, the deification of Man. And the other was born in heaven, the glorification of God!

…I'd like to see some people repent on biblical terms again…. Dear friends, there's only one reason, one reason for a sinner to repent and that's because Jesus Christ deserves the worship and adoration and the love and the obedience of his heart…. If the only reason he repents is so that he'll go to heaven, it's nothing but trying to make a deal or a bargain with God…. I believe that the only ones [to] whom God actually witnesses by His Spirit that [they] are born of Him, are the people, whether they say it or not, that come to Jesus Christ and say something like this: "Lord Jesus, I'm going to obey You and love You and serve You and do what You want me to do as long as I live, even if I go to hell at the end of the road,[2] simply because You are worthy to be loved and obeyed and served, and I'm not trying to make a deal with You!"

…My only reason for being is for the glory of God in Jesus Christ. …Let's be done, once and for all, with utilitarian Christianity that makes God a *means*, instead of *the glorious End* that He is.

Know that I believe the saved will go to heaven if they die,[3] and we should praise God with thanksgiving for this. *But heaven is not the goal; the praise is.* First Peter 2:9-10 explains we were shown mercy to become God's kingly priesthood, *"so that you may proclaim the excellencies of Him* who has called you out of darkness into His marvelous light" (NASB). *The goal of the gospel is God's glory in the believer* (2 Thess. 2:14, more on pp. 84-89).

Since first falling in love with that Reidhead sermon, I became a Christian Hedonist.[4] Now I cringe at Reidhead's

---

2. I assume, on good grounds, that Reidhead did not think this was possible, but he dared say it because of Paul's willingness to be cursed and cut off from Christ, if God would then be glorified in unbelieving Israel (Rom. 9:1-4, cf. Ex. 32:32).

3. Temporarily, until they come back to earth with Jesus (1 Thess. 4:14-17).

disjunctions between the glory of God and the happiness of Man, which I believe are actually one and the same. God is most glorified in me when I find my happiness in Him. Therefore, God did not intend my happiness to be a "by-product" of glorifying Him. No, God intended my happiness in Him to be *the means* of glorifying Him. How could it be otherwise? Would He be shown to be as glorious as He is if I did my duties and recited God-centered theology with no sense of wonder and delight in Him? Furthermore, how could I fulfill my duties without obeying commands like Psalm 37:4, "Delight yourself in Yahweh"? The Epilogue to *Part One* will stress the truth of this paragraph, but I wanted to log my objection to my own Reidhead quote here, so we could pick out that bone, and still savor the marinated chicken.

That is to say, even Christian Hedonists can amen Reidhead's strong call to make God the end and goal of the gospel, rather than merely the means of getting to heaven. The one who taught me about the pursuit of pleasure in God, John Piper, wrote an entire book to make that point. In *God Is the Gospel*, Piper puts it like this:

> The critical question for our generation – and for every generation – is this: If you could have heaven, with no sickness, and with all the friends you ever had on earth, and all the food you ever liked, and all the leisure activities you ever enjoyed, and all the natural beauties you ever saw, all the physical pleasures you ever tasted, and no human conflict or any natural disasters, could you be satisfied with heaven, if Christ were not there?[5]

---

4. Hedonism is the pursuit of pleasure. I believe you cannot help pursuing pleasure because God wired you to pursue pleasure and find true satisfaction in Him. He did so because, when God is your greatest delight, He looks glorious, as He is. See the article by John Piper, "Christian Hedonism: Forgive the Label, But Don't Miss the Truth," 1 Jan 1995 (desiringGod.org/articles/christian-hedonism), or the sermon "God Is Most Glorified in Us When We Are Most Satisfied in Him," 13 Oct 2012 (desiringGod.org/messages/god-is-most-glorified-in-us-when-we-are-most-satisfied-in-him), or the conference message "Christian Hedonism with Questions and Answers," 1 Jan 1998 (desiringGod.org/messages/christian-

Later he adds: "…people who would be happy in heaven if Christ were not there, will not be there. The gospel is not a way to get people to heaven; it is a way to get people to God"[6] (cf. 1 Pet. 3:18). Piper labors for us to see that we can share true facets of the gospel and yet leave out the ultimate. For example:

> Why is justification good news?… A person may answer, "Being forgiven is good news because I don't want to go to hell." Or a person may answer, "Being forgiven is good news because a guilty conscience is a horrible thing, and I get great relief when I believe my sins are forgiven." Or a person may answer, "I want to go to heaven." But then we must ask why they want to go to heaven. They might answer, "Because the alternative is painful." Or "because my deceased wife is there." Or "because there will be a new heaven and a new earth where justice and beauty will finally be everywhere." What's wrong with these answers? … What's wrong with them is that they do not treat God as the final and highest good of the gospel. They do not express a supreme desire to be with God. God was not even mentioned. Only his gifts were mentioned. These gifts are precious. But they are not God.[7]

In these quotes, Piper sounds similar to Reidhead, yet he properly, Biblically, brings together the glorification of God and the happiness of Man:

> Until the gospel *events* of Good Friday and Easter and the gospel promises of justification and eternal life lead you to behold and embrace God *himself* as your highest joy, you have not embraced the gospel of God. You have embraced some of his gifts. You have rejoiced over some of his rewards. You have marveled at some of his miracles. But you have not yet been

hedonism-with-questions-and-answers), or the book *Desiring God: Meditations of a Christian Hedonist,* Revised Edition (Colorado Springs: Multnomah, 2011) – note its appendix – or the condensed version, *The Dangerous Duty of Delight: Daring to Make God Your Greatest Treasure* (Colorado Springs: Multnomah, 2011).

5. *God Is the Gospel: Meditations on God's Love as the Gift of Himself* (Wheaton, IL: Crossway, 2005), 15.

6. *Ibid.,* 47.

7. *Ibid.,* 44, 45.

awakened to why the gifts, the rewards, and the miracles have come. They have come for one great reason: that you might behold forever the glory of God in Christ, and by beholding become the kind of person who delights in God above all things, and by delighting display his supreme beauty and worth with ever-increasing brightness and bliss forever.[8]

My heart swells at that truth, especially because I have made the mistakes Piper warns against. I have shared true aspects of the gospel without God as the goal. I have offered a ticket to heaven to sinners who had no intention to forsake sin and embrace God for His glory. They wanted a Savior (on the sideline) without a Lord. In my own repentance I now say: to be saved, a sinner must repent and submit to the Lordship of Jesus, denying self for God's glory in Christ.[9] *The gospel is not ultimately about self-preservation, but God-exultation.*

The angel in Revelation 14:6-7 summarizes the "eternal gospel" as "Fear God and *give him glory,* because the hour of his judgment has come, and *worship him* who made heaven and earth, the sea and the springs of water." Some have understandably questioned if this "eternal gospel" is different from the gospel of Jesus Christ (since it does not mention His Name or work), but no different gospel exists (Gal. 1:6-9).[10] This passage does not intend to represent the fullness of gospel *content,* but the *response* to it, which is its *goal:* every nation and tribe and language and people glorifying and worshiping their Creator.

As Reidhead sermonized, Revelation 16:9 describes repentance as a change from denying God glory to giving God

---

8. *Ibid.,* 37-38. He also writes, "When I say that *God Is the Gospel* I mean that the highest, best, final, decisive good of the gospel, without which no other gifts would be good, is the glory of God in the face of Christ revealed for our everlasting enjoyment. The saving love of God is God's commitment to do everything necessary to enthrall us with what is most deeply and durably satisfying, namely himself" (13). "The acid test of biblical God-centeredness – and faithfulness to the gospel – is this: Do you feel more loved because God makes much of you, or because, at the cost of his Son, he enables you to enjoy making much of him forever?" (11).

glory.[11] Likewise, Isaiah 56:6 described the motivation for those among the nations who would "join themselves to Yahweh, to minister to Him, *to love the Name of Yahweh*, and to be His servants" (cf. Ps. 5:11, 119:132). This should be our heart and the aim of our gospel invitations because we know the glory of His Name is God's goal and the greatest worth.

The gospel is "the gospel of the glory of the happy God" (1 Tim. 1:11, AT). According to 2 Corinthians 4:4-6:

> …the god of this age has blinded the minds of unbelievers for the light of *the gospel of the glory of Christ*, who is the image of God, not to shine into them. [5]For we are not proclaiming ourselves, but Jesus Christ as Lord, and ourselves as your servants *for Jesus' sake*. [6]Because God, who said, "Out of darkness, light will shine," shone in our hearts for the light of the knowledge of *the glory of God in the face of Jesus Christ*" (AT).

Piper writes, "Satan is not mainly interested in causing us misery. He is mainly interested in making Christ look bad…. The gospel is God's instrument for liberating people from exulting in self to exulting in Christ. Therefore Satan hates the gospel."[12] As we saw with Job, this war is about the glory of God. The gospel is the power of God unto salvation because by it God speaks a Creation-level miracle (like Gen. 1:3, quoted), conquering the darkness of sin and Satan and giving new-heart eyes to see and savor His beauty in Jesus.[13] Our receiving and sharing the gospel should be "for Jesus' sake" so that all may see the glory of God in the face of Christ.

---

9.   Rom. 10:9-13, Mt. 3:2, 4:17; Lk. 5:8-11, 14:25-33; Mt. 10:37-38; Mt. 16:24, Mk. 8:34, Lk. 9:23

10. I agree with Grant R. Osborne's treatment in *Revelation*, BECNT (Grand Rapids, MI: Baker Academic, 2002), 534-537.

11. Cf. 11:13. Jer. 13:15-17 defines repentance as rejecting pride and giving glory to Yahweh.

12. *God Is the Gospel*, 62.

13. *Ibid*. Cf. Chapter 4, esp. pp. 74-76.

THE ETERNAL PURPOSE OF SALVATION

In considering the purposes of God and especially the purpose of redemption, we perhaps cannot find Scriptures more purposeful than Ephesians 1:3-14 (AT), which reveal what and why God predestined before the founding of the world:

> [3]Blessed be, the God and Father of, our Lord Jesus Christ, the One, having blessed us with every spiritual blessing in the heavenly realms in Christ, [4]even as He chose us in Him before the, founding of the, world for, us to be holy and blameless before Him in love, [5]having predetermined us for adoption unto Himself through Jesus Christ, according to the pleasure of, His will, [6]*unto the, praise of the, glory of, His grace,* with, which He graced us in the Beloved, [7]in whom we have redemption through His blood, the forgiveness of, transgressions, according to the wealth of, *His grace,* [8]which He caused to abound to us in all wisdom and understanding, [9]having made known to, us the secret of, His will, according to His pleasure, which He purposed in Him [10]with a view to the, economy of, the fullness of, times, *to head up all things, in Christ,* the things, in the heavens and the things, upon the earth, in Him, [11]in whom also we were allotted, having been predetermined according to the purpose of, the One who is, working all things, according to the plan of, His will, [12]for us to be *unto the praise of, His glory,* the ones, having first hoped in Christ, [13]in whom also you, having heard the word of, truth, the gospel of, your salvation, in whom also having believed, you were sealed with, the Holy Spirit of, promise, [14]who is the, downpayment of, our inheritance, unto the, redemption of, the possession, *unto the praise of, His glory!*

The Old Testament precedent for a benediction was one simple statement (e.g., Ps. 66:20). Here, uniquely, Paul composed one long sentence of 202 words in the Greek because he was worshiping and seeking to evoke in the readers a mental and emotional response of humble, joyful worship for such a gracious, Trinitarian redemption. The sovereign *Father* chose and predestined us in the *Son*, who redeemed us by His blood, and the *Spirit* sealed us until God takes full possession of us in holy love. In this the benediction plumbs the depths of eternity past and scales the heights of eternity future with the Cross of Christ at the center.

In this densely packed theology-in-doxology, Paul emphasizes the overarching, pre-ordained purpose of God in our salvation: to the praise of the glory of His grace, to the praise of His glory, to the praise of His glory (vv. 6, 12, 14). The first instance singles out grace,[14] which is central to the glory He defined in Exodus 34:6-7, "Yahweh, Yahweh, a God merciful and *gracious…* bearing iniquity…." We learn in Ephesians 1 that it pleased God (v. 5) to create a world in which the apex of His glory is the glory of His grace manifest in the slaughter of His beloved Son for the redemption of His chosen people.[15] Bankrupt in spirit, we deserved nothing good. Dead in our transgressions (2:1, 5), we contributed nothing to our salvation.[16] We simply received the gift (2:8-9). And the Giver gets all the glory.[17] And we get the joy, the Spirit enlivening us to share in the Son's joyful love for the Father and Father's pleasure in the Son, our gracious Redeemer.

---

14. And Paul immediately emphasizes grace: "with which He graced us" (v. 6, AT). Then he grounds our redemption and forgiveness in "the wealth of His grace" (v. 7). He also interrupts the flow of the sentence in 2:5-6 to emphatically interject: "by grace you have been and are saved" (as though he could not wait for the formal statement in 2:8). Also, in 2:7 the purpose of salvation is "in order that in the coming ages He may display the surpassing wealth of His grace in kindness toward us in Christ Jesus."

15. Cf. John Piper, *Spectacular Sins: And Their Global Purpose in the Glory of Christ* (Wheaton, IL: Crossway, 2008), 12.

16. On our inability as dead, see also Gen. 2:17, Ezek. 36:26-27, 37:1-14, Eph. 4:18, Mt. 8:21, 23:37-38, Jn. 3:3-8, 5:24-25, 6:53, and 6:63 (AT), "The Spirit is the One making alive; *the flesh is benefitting absolutely nothing*. The words I have spoken to you are Spirit, and they are life."

17. We realize why Paul so tenaciously guarded grace apart from works when we see that *sola gratia* (grace alone) protects *soli Deo gloria* (to the glory of God alone). I.e., God alone gets the glory for a salvation that is by grace alone. And Paul is above all concerned that God alone receives the glory due Him.

Therefore, the ultimate reason for you – for your history
and for your eternity – is to praise the glory of God's grace in
His beloved Son.[18] Are you? Are you living for the praise of His
glory? There is no greater goal. No greater joy. He is worthy!

---

18. In addition, note Paul's prayer for "the Father of glory" to enlighten the eyes of our
hearts to know "the wealth of the glory of His inheritance in the holy ones" (1:17-
19). What assurance: God is committed to us because He stands to gain glory from
us, the highest value in the universe, to which He is unswervingly committed.

CHAPTER FOUR

DISCIPLES FOR GLORY

Before Jesus died and ascended to His throne as a resurrected, glorified God-Man, He told His disciples that He would send the promised gift of the Holy Spirit.[1] Christ defined *the Spirit's mission: "He will glorify Me"* (Jn. 16:14). We now see that *the Father, Son, and Spirit share the same goal: the glory of the Triune God in the preeminence of Christ.*

FAITH IN THE CONTEXT OF GOD'S GLORY

We receive the Holy Spirit by repenting from our sinfulness and believing the gospel: that Jesus is God the Son, who died for our sins, was raised, and is coming again to judge the world.[2] We are saved by grace through faith, and we are being made holy by grace through faith,[3] so faith is fairly important.

As I have asserted about everything, faith, too, should be viewed in the context of God's glory. Faith is a response to God's

---

1. Lk. 24:49; Jn. 4:10-14, 7:37-39, 14:15-27, 16:7-15; Acts 1:8, 2:33; 1 Cor. 15:45
2. N. 9, p. 67; Eph. 1:13-14, Acts 5:32, 17:31; 1 Cor. 15:1-4; Ps. 96:13, Rom. 2:16

self-revelation (Rom. 10:17). God manifests His glory through word or mighty deed, and we respond: "Amen. Yes. True. I love it." Faith is the substantiation of God's revelation (trusting who He is, so as to make it personally real, Heb. 11:1). God is revealing His *worth*, and the believing are those making Him their greatest *treasure*.

We see such a requirement for faith throughout the Gospels. Jesus did not come to gather crowds of self-centered converts. He called, taught, and befriended God-glorifying disciples (Jn. 15:8, 14-17 and context). He sent the selfish away with His hard words that only the ones who forsake everything – even family, even their own lives – are truly disciples who will be saved.[4] Such a hard line makes sense when we consider that God, manifest in Christ, is the greatest worth; therefore, to treat Him as anything less is not faith.

In John 6, so-called "disciples" were following Jesus to get miraculously free bread (v. 26). When called to be true disciples, they stopped following and "went away unto the things they had left behind" (v. 66, AT). They treasured their old lives more than Jesus. He offered the Twelve a chance to leave, too (v. 67), but Peter represented their faith with his response: "Lord, to whom would we go away? You have the words of eternal life, and we ourselves have believed and have come to know that You Yourself are the Holy One of God" (Jn. 6:68-69, AT). True disciples are the ones who see that Jesus is one-of-a-kind, the only holy, infinitely perfect Son of God. Where else would we go? What else would we do? Nothing compares to Jesus Christ! This treasuring of Christ is what constituted their faith and made them disciples, willing to follow and obey.

Jesus told them, "You yourselves did not choose Me, but I Myself chose you and appointed you that you yourselves may go

---

3.   Eph. 2:8-9, Acts 18:27; Gal. 3:1-5 (esp. v. 3), Col. 2:6, 1 Cor. 15:10

4.   Lk. 5:11, 9:23-27, 9:57-62, 14:25-33; Mt. 10:37-38; see *Introduction to Disciple-*

and bear fruit..." (Jn. 15:16, AT, cf. 6:70). God's plan for disciples is to place the Spirit of Christ in them so that through their faith His life will manifest through them (the metaphor of producing fruit). That manifestation of God's life is glory. Jesus said, "In this My Father is glorified: that you may be bearing much fruit and become My disciples" (15:8, AT). *Only God-glorifying fruit-bearers are disciples of Jesus.*[5]

Jesus said the pursuit of glory from man makes faith impossible: "How can you believe, when you receive glory from one another and do not seek the glory that comes from the only God?" (Jn. 5:44).[6] John also commented later about pseudo-faith that did not confess Christ because "they loved the glory that comes from man more than the glory that comes from God" (12:43).

Not seeking God's glory inhibits faith, but seeking God's glory strengthens faith. Abraham "grew strong in his faith, having given glory to God and having become fully convinced that what He promised, He is also powerful to do" (Rom. 4:20-21, AT). Substantiating God's worth (His holiness, power, faithfulness, graciousness, and justice) and worshiping Him for it, giving Him glory – this grows our faith.

Faith Working through Love

Paul said, "The only thing that counts is faith expressing itself through love" (Gal. 5:6b NIV). Jesus affirmed the greatest command is to "love the Lord your God with your whole heart and with your whole soul and with your whole mind" (Mt. 22:37, AT). God demands (and deserves) wholehearted devotion. Nursing competing affections is not loving from faith that sees

---

making, 5-8 (ProjectOne28.com/i2dm).

5. Fruitless "followers" will be cut off from Christ and thrown into the fire (Jn. 15:2, 6). In John 15:8, "show" (NIV) or "prove" (ESV, NASB) are loose glosses for *ginomai*, lit., "become."

6. More on pp. 86-89 about how we're meant to receive glory, but from God, not Man.

God's incomparable worth in Christ. Love, like everything else, must be defined in terms of glory.

What is love? At least toward humans, love is not simply doing whatever makes the loved one happy (immediately). My kids always, always want candy. It would make them happy for me to give them candy every time they asked (for a little while, until it would make them sick). Even though they ask so sweetly, and even though it would make them happy, I know it is not for their best, so I often say, "No." Therefore, I teach that love is desiring and seeking what is best for someone.[7] Elaborating to be more specific, for humans, to love is:

> (1) to see someone's worth,
> (2) to delight in that worth,
> (3) to desire the best for that person, and
> (4) to act for that best at any cost.

This definition works both for loving God and loving neighbors, but we will focus here on loving God.[8]

(1) Seeing God's worth is the first step because love comes out of faith; it is a fruit of the Spirit (Gal. 5:22), borne by abiding faith (3:5). Faith and then love come out of seeing God's glory, including the glory of His love:[9] "We love because he first loved us" (1 Jn. 4:19, cf. v. 10).[10] If someone does not love God, it is

---

7. After years of teaching this, assuming originality, I saw a similar sentence already highlighted in John Piper, *Don't Waste Your Life* (Wheaton, IL: Crossway Books, 2003), 33, so I obviously should credit Pastor John for setting me on this track. After writing steps one and two below, I found confirmation in Martin Luther's Heidelberg Thesis 28, "...The love of man comes into being through that which is pleasing to it."

8. For the application of this definition to the second greatest commandment, "Love your neighbor as yourself," see the audio and notes to Spencer Stewart, "Loving God and Loving Each Other for the Glory of God," 10 Apr 2011 (ProjectOne28. com/loving-each-other). See ProjectOne28.com/scougal for a seventeenth century quote from Henry Scougal, which I found after writing and preaching this and was pleasantly surprised by the similarities in his definition of love for God.

9. I write "the glory of His love" because it is featured in Yahweh's own definition of His glory in Exodus 34:6-7.

because he is blinded and cannot see God's glory (2 Cor. 4:4). Seeing compels loving. And we cannot see the glory of God in Christ without being born from above (Jn. 3:3-8). Dead people cannot see. God must give us spiritual eyes to see[11] by causing us to be born again through the word of the gospel,[12] unblinding us and shining the light of His glory into our hearts.

(2) God shows us Himself, and we respond by believing and delighting in Him. I chose the word "delight" because, besides its Biblical support,[13] I wanted to add a word less watered-down in our culture than "believe." Believe is an adequate word, for sure (and it is already entailed in the Biblical kind of *seeing* in step one of this definition). But too many stop at some pseudo-faith that intellectually agrees with some facts (or assumptions or falsehoods). Even the demons "believe" (Jas. 2:19). In fact, the demons featured in the events in the Gospels possessed more spontaneous and accurate "belief" than anybody else (e.g., Lk 4:34, 41). But they did not delight in what they knew.[14] Disciples delight: "You are worthy! Infinitely worthy! There's no one else like You! No other God loved me before the foundation of the world and became a God-Man to die for my sins and put His Spirit in me. Thank you!" And this is where emotional

---

10. This definition fits how God loves us, with an amendment for point one: (1) though we are unworthy enemies, He chose us by grace, His unmerited favor, (2) delights in us, e.g., Isa. 62:5, Zeph. 3:17, (3) desires our best, which is Himself, (4) and He acted at the highest cost by dying to give us the best: Himself, His Spirit. Martin Luther celebrated this difference in reactionary human love and merciful divine love: "The love of God does not find, but creates, that which is pleasing to it. The love of man comes into being through that which is pleasing to it" (Heidelberg Thesis 28). Regarding footnote 2 on page 5, God's *love* can be centered on His glory in us because His glory is what is best for us. Acting for His glory in us means giving us the best (Himself) at the highest cost (Himself as propitiation), which is therefore the greatest love (Jn. 15:13), for which He is praised.

11. Dt. 29:4, Jn. 1:4, 8:12, 9:39; 2 Cor. 4:4-6; Eph. 1:18, Rev. 3:17-18, Isa. 42:7, Lk. 4:18, Acts 26:18

12. 1 Pet. 1:3, 23-25; Jas. 1:18

13. Isa. 55:2, 58:14; Job 22:26; Jer. 15:16; Mal. 3:1; Neh. 1:11; Rom. 7:22; Ps. 1:2, 37:4, 40:8, 111:2; 119:4, 16, 24, 70, 77, 92, 143, 174

14. See the Jonathan Edwards quote on page 98.

affection comes into play: "You're perfect! You don't need to change anything about You. I delight in You. I delight in Your perfection and Your everlasting love! I love everything You are! I adore You!"

(3) Sight and delight naturally lead to desiring what is best for God. What is best for God? Himself! The best thing for God is for Him to act in faithfulness to who He is, so that He displays His glory and receives the praise of which He is worthy.[15] If I truly, delightfully believe God is ultimately worthy of everything, I will be jealous for Him to get what He deserves – from me and from everyone and everything.

(4) If I desire God's best – for Him to be glorified – then I surely must act. I want to do something, and I am in a position to do something. To begin with, I am made to be a true worshiper, so I am able to praise. And I am an image-bearer who can display His glory so others can see and praise. Faith through love is not faith through love unless it produces obedient action. Even the Son of God showed His love for the Father through submissive obedience (Jn. 14:31). Jesus told His disciples:

> If you love Me, you will keep My commandments.… [21]The ,one, having My commands and keeping them, that ,one, is the ,one, loving Me; and the ,one, loving Me will be loved by My Father, and I will love Him, and I will manifest Myself ,to, him.… [23]Whoever loves Me will keep My word, and My Father will love him, and We will come to him, and We will

---

15. The definition of love offered in this section is confirmed by the nature of the love of the Triune God. "God is love" (1 Jn. 4:8, 16), and God does not change (Mal. 3:6); therefore, God has always been love. Even before any created things existed to which God could direct His love, He was loving the only Being to love: Himself – the Father loving the Son and the Spirit, the Son loving the Father and the Spirit, and the Spirit loving the Father and the Son! What raging love! Cf. Jn. 17:24. And we have seen that each Member of the Trinity knows the worth of the "Others," delights in Them, and seeks Their glory. The Father seeks to glorify the Son, the Son to glorify the Father (through obedience), and the Spirit to glorify the Son. Intra-Trinitarian love is expressed as passion for glory. I believe I received this definition of love as "passion for glory" years ago from Brent Curtis and John Eldredge, *The Sacred Romance: Drawing Closer to the Heart of God* (Thomas Nelson, 1997), perhaps 158.

make ˏOurˏ abode with him. [24]The ˏoneˏ not loving Me does not keep My words… (Jn. 14:15, 21, 23-24, AT).

If you are not obeying Jesus, then you are not loving Jesus. (I do not mean obeying perfectly, but intentionally, increasingly.)[16] If you love Jesus, then you obey, because you want to please Him (2 Cor. 5:9), and you want Him to receive the glory He deserves – not just sometimes, but always.

EVERYTHING FOR GLORY

To believe in God and love God means to see His worth, delight in Him as our greatest treasure, and therefore, do everything for His glory. This is confirmed by explicit commands in Scripture:

> "Do everything in love" (1 Cor. 16:14 NIV).

> "Therefore, whether you are eating, or whether you are drinking, or whether you are doing anything, *be doing all things for the glory of God!*" (1 Cor. 10:31, AT).

To love is to live for what is best, God's glory. We are commanded to be doing all things for His glory; thus to do anything for a lesser goal is to miss the mark, to sin.

Christ *died* for us, so that we would *live* for Him:

> For the love of Christ controls us, having concluded this, that one died for all, therefore all died; and He died for all, *so that* they who live might *no longer live for themselves, but for Him* who died and rose again on their behalf (2 Cor. 5:14-15 NASB).

Jesus commanded us to *be praying first of all for the glory of God's Name:* "Hallowed be Your Name… on earth even as in heaven" (Mt. 6:9-10, AT).[17] Jesus also promised *He will answer*

---

16. See ProjectOne.com/sanctification.

17. See *The Model Prayer: Jesus Said, "Be Praying in This Manner…"* (ProjectOne28.com/prayer).

prayers to glorify God: "Whatever you ask in my name, this I will do, *that* the Father may be glorified in the Son" (Jn. 14:13).

Jesus commanded us to *do good works, so that God will be glorified:* "Let your light shine before others, so that they may see your good works and give glory to your Father who is in heaven" (Mt. 5:16). Peter concurred: "Keep your conduct among the Gentiles honorable, so that when they speak against you as evildoers, they may see your good deeds and glorify God on the day of visitation" (1 Pet. 2:12).

The famous saying goes, "Preach the gospel always, and if necessary, use words."[18] The point about living out Christ is well made, but the phrase "if necessary" could be misleading. It is always necessary. "Gospel" is good *news;* news must be proclaimed.[19] Merely seeing a believer's good deeds cannot enable an unbeliever to glorify God on the day of visitation, as Peter motivated us. The unbeliever must repent and believe the gospel of Jesus Christ, but how can he believe unless he has heard (Rom. 10:14-15)? Faith comes by hearing the *word* of Christ (10:17). Therefore, our good works for God's glory must be accompanied by an articulation of "the gospel of the glory of Christ." Otherwise, we usurp credit for the good works, which He deserves, and the lost remain lost. We are also commanded:

> "And whatever you do, in word or deed, *do everything in the name of the Lord Jesus*, giving thanks to God the Father through him" (Col. 3:17).[20]

Let us not become sidetracked with arguments for *either* good deeds *or* gospel proclamation.[21] Scripture commands both.

---

18. This is often falsely attributed to St. Francis of Assisi. See Garrett Kell's blog post (garrettkell.com/what-st-francis-really-said-about-preaching-the-gospel/) for the actual quote that probably gave rise to the untrue truism.

19. Consider 1 Cor. 1:21. D. A. Carson treats this subject well in "What Is the Gospel? Revisited," in *For the Fame of God's Name: Essays in Honor of John Piper*, ed. Sam Storms and Justin Taylor (Wheaton, IL: Crossway, 2010), 158 (also notes 11-13).

20. Likewise, it was prophesied that we would "walk in the Name of Yahweh our God" (Mic. 4:5, cf. Zech. 10:12).

Unbelievers need both – to see the glory of God manifested through our lives and to hear that this glory comes through Christ.[22] Proclaiming the gospel is one of the good deeds (!) God has prepared for us, and what a privilege to show Christ and proclaim Christ in all things by His Spirit. As imitators of God (Eph. 5:1), who does everything for the glory of His Name, may we do everything in His Name and for His Name.

The motivation for evangelism is to partner with God in seeking true worshipers (Jn. 4:23-24). One of John Piper's famous aphorisms is "Missions exists because worship doesn't."[23] The Spirit commands us through the psalmist: *"Declare His glory among the nations*, His marvelous works among all the peoples! For great is Yahweh, and greatly to be praised..." (Ps. 96:3-4). Seven centuries before our King commanded us to disciple all the nations (Mt. 28:18-20), it was prophesied that He would send His people to nations far away, who "have not heard my fame or seen my glory. And they shall *declare my glory among the nations.* And they shall bring all your brothers from the nations as an offering to Yahweh..." so that "all flesh shall come and worship before me."[24] Paul viewed his ministry to Gentiles as fulfillment of that prophecy in Isaiah (see Rom. 15:16) and explained the divine goal of his team's apostleship as "unto the obedience of faith among all the peoples *for the sake of His Name"* (1:5, AT).

Concerning the glorifying obedience of faith, the Spirit reasoned and commanded, in the context of sexual purity, "You are not your own... You have been bought with a price:

---

21. See the author's "Righteousness and Justice: The Foundation of God's Throne," 16 Oct 2011 (ProjectOne28.com/justice).

22. That is the model of the apostles, who immediately gave glory to Jesus for the miracles done in His Name (e.g., Acts 3:11-16).

23. John Piper, *Let the Nations Be Glad: The Supremacy of God in Missions*, Third Edition (Grand Rapids, MI: Baker Academic, 2010), 15. I also highly recommend his conference message, "Let the Peoples Praise You, O God, Let All the Peoples Praise You!" (ProjectOne28.com/jp-on-ps67).

24. Isa. 66:18-23, cf. 12:3-6, 24:14-15; Zeph. 2:11, 3:9-10; Ps. 86:9, 102:15.

therefore *glorify God in your body"* (1 Cor. 6:19-20 NASB). Paul prayed the Philippian believers would be "filled with the fruit of righteousness that comes through Jesus Christ, to the glory and praise of God" (1:11). He prayed God would make the Thessalonians worthy of His calling and fulfill their every resolve for good and every work of faith by His power, "so that the *name* of our Lord Jesus may be *glorified"* in them (2 Thess. 1:12).

We are encouraged to operate in our spiritual gifts by God's power *"in order that in* all things *God may be being glorified through Jesus Christ, to whom is the glory and might into the ages of the ages; amen!"* (1 Pet. 4:11, AT). All things for God's glory through Christ! All things!

Fruit-bearing disciples seeking the glory of God in Christ will even endure persecution to the point of death – because God's glory is worth more than this temporary life. Now we have reached the final clause in our definition of love: at any cost.[25] Jesus promised His disciples: the world "will deliver you up to tribulation and put you to death, and you will be hated by all nations *for my name's sake.* And then many will [be stumbled]…. But the one who endures to the end will be saved" (Mt. 24:9-10, 13). When the heat comes because of Jesus' Name, many will shy away and fall away (Mt. 13:6, 21), but true disciples consider persecution an "opportunity to bear witness" (Lk. 21:13) to the Name of Jesus at any cost. The apostles, after being arrested and beaten, "left the presence of the council, *rejoicing* that they were counted worthy to suffer dishonor *for the name"* (Acts 5:41).[26] John later honored brothers who had "gone out *for the sake of the name"* (3 Jn. 1:7). Peter later exhorted:

---

25. Definition on p. 74. Jesus loved for glory at the highest cost (Jn. 15:13, 1 Jn. 3:16).

26. This passage (among many) declares that Jesus is Yahweh in flesh. Jews after OT times began to say *Adonai* ("Lord") instead of *Yahweh* to protect against taking the Name in vain (Ex. 20:7; see Chapter Two of *Part Two* for more). Eventually, instead of *Adonai,* they replaced it with *hashem,* saying simply, "the Name." Jesus is "the Name" (cf. Lev. 24:11, Phil. 2:9-11; 3 Jn. 7). From Hans Beitenhard, "Name," *NIDNT,* 2:652, 654.

> If you are insulted for the name of Christ, you are blessed, because *the Spirit of glory* and of God rests upon you. …if anyone suffers as a Christian, let him not be ashamed, but let him *glorify God in that name* (1 Pet. 4:14, 16).

That from the disciple who heard Jesus prophesy "what kind of death he was to glorify God" (Jn. 21:19). The resurrected Jesus commended the Ephesians for enduring persecution for His Name's sake (Rev. 2:3). He also commissioned Paul by saying, "I will show him how much he must suffer for the sake of my name" (Acts 9:16).

Paul, in prison, "ready to die... for the name of the Lord Jesus" (Acts 21:13), wrote: "It is my eager expectation and hope that... with full courage now as always Christ will be magnified in my body, whether by life or by death. For to me, to live is Christ, and to die is gain" (Phil. 1:20-21, AT). Until a disciple dies, he lives Christ – manifests Christ's glory through the loving obedience of faith. John Piper quoted Paul's confession and then preached:

> Christ is most magnified in us when are most satisfied in him when we lose everything but him…. How do you make Christ look magnificent when you're dying? Answer: You say, "Gain!" If death takes everything and leaves only him, you say, "Gain!" And when you say that, the demons gnash their teeth in hell. When dying Christians say, "Gain!" the angels rejoice. Christ is magnified by being preferred above everything that life can offer.[27]

Even if we die, we win. "Whoever believes in Me, though he die, yet shall he live" (Jn. 11:25). Immediately entering the joy of our Master in His paradise,[28] we win. Our bodies will be resurrected at Christ's second coming, so if God wills that we use our bodies here to glorify Him in martyrdom, then may He

---

27. "Treasuring Christ and the Call to Suffer: Part 2," 6 Sept 2007 (desiringGod.org/messages/treasuring-christ-and-the-call-to-suffer-part-2).

28. Mt. 25:21, 23; Lk. 23:43; Rev. 2:7

be glorified indeed! When we seemingly lose, we are more than conquerors (Rom. 8:37). Just as Satan's bruising of Jesus' heel secured the crushing of Satan's head,[29] Revelation 12:11 portrays the Antichrist's conquering of the saints (13:7) as the means by which the saints conquer Satan:

> And they have conquered him by the blood of the Lamb and by the word of their testimony, for they loved not their lives even unto death.

This plumbs the depths of "the cost" of discipleship.[30] If we love our lives so that we keep them for ourselves, rather than lose them to bear witness to Christ's incomparable worth, then we are not really disciples (Jn. 12:23-26). But if we love His Name more than our families and more than our very lives, then Christ is glorified in us, and He will glorify us in His presence (cf. Mt. 10:32, Rev. 3:5). Romans 8:17-18 (AT) expounds on the truth that believers are adopted children of God:

> And if children, also heirs – indeed, heirs of God, and co-heirs with Christ, if we suffer with Him, in order that we also may be glorified with Him. [18]Because I reckon that the sufferings of the present time are not worth being compared to the glory about to be revealed into us.

Paul, whose sufferings we would not describe as light, testified: "the momentary lightness of our tribulation *is producing* for us *an eternal weight of glory* beyond all comparison..." (2 Cor. 4:17, AT).[31]

HOPE OF GLORY

We are motivated to lay down our lives and do everything in the Name of Jesus for the glory of God because of conviction

---

29. Gen. 3:15

30. E.g., Lk. 14:25-33 (see *Introduction to Disciple-making* at ProjectOne28.com/i2dm – esp. pp. 5-7).

31. I cannot recommend highly enough the conference message by John Piper on this passage, "The Glory of God in the Sight of Eternity," as well as the version of the

of His worth, thankfulness for His redeeming sacrifice, desire to know Him by sharing in His sufferings,[32] and hope of future glory. See how Paul described his ministry in Colossians 1:25-27 (AT):

> to fulfill the word of God, [26]the secret having been hidden from the ages and from the generations, but now has been manifested to His holy ones, [27]to whom God wanted to make known among the peoples what is, *the wealth of the glory of this secret, which is Christ in you [plural], the hope of glory....*

Christ is in each believer individually, forming Himself in us collectively as His Body.[33] Christ is the Glory of God. Therefore, the Glory of God is in us and will fill us completely (Eph. 1:23).

Therefore, "we exult [boast, rejoice triumphantly] in hope of the glory of God" (Rom. 5:2 NASB). In one sense, this is the confident expectation of seeing the glory of God. No one but the Son has ever seen God the Father as He is, but *we* will see Him.[34] Now, our physical eyes could not handle the glory of the God who dwells in unapproachable light (1 Tim. 6:16). We cannot even stare at the sun in its strength, and that is a shadowy parable that will fade away when God displays the fullness of His glory on the new earth.[35] But our physical eyes in our resurrected bodies will be able to see God's glory unfiltered, and what a joy that will be!

But this is not all. We will not only *see* the glory of God; we will *be* the glory of God. Before the foundation of the world, God planned to fill all things with His glory by filling the earth with subduing and ruling image-bearers (Gen. 1:26-28). In fact, Man is purposed to *be* "the image and the glory of God" (1 Cor.

Shane & Shane song, "Though You Slay Me," which incorporates some audio from Piper's message. Both can be found through ProjectOne28.com/suffering.

32. Phil. 3:10

33. E.g., Gal. 4:19, 1 Cor. 12:12, Eph. 1:22-23

34. 1 Tim. 6:16; Jn. 1:18, 6:46; Col. 1:15; 1 Jn. 4:12, 3:2; Mt. 5:8; 1 Cor. 13:10-12

35. Isa. 24:23, 60:19-20, Zech. 14:6-7, Rev. 21:23, 22:5

11:7). Adam failed, but in Christ, this plan will succeed. Paul and his apostolic team imparted "a secret and hidden wisdom of God, which God decreed before the ages *for our glory"* (1 Cor. 2:7). Romans 9:23 speaks of "the riches of his glory for vessels of mercy, which he has prepared beforehand *for glory."* Those who receive the mercy of God in Christ were prepared before the ages to be glorified:

> ROMANS 8:29-30 (AT)
> Because whom He foreknew, He also predestined to be, *conformed to the image of His Son,* for Him to be the firstborn among many brothers; [30]and whom He predestined, these He also called, and whom He called, these He also declared righteous, and whom He declared righteous, *these He also glorified.*

Through the suffering of God's One-of-a-kind Son, the Father was "bringing many sons to glory" (Heb. 2:10). Paul wrote to the Thessalonians: "...God chose you as the firstfruits to be saved, through sanctification by the Spirit and belief in the truth. To this he called you through our gospel, so that you may *obtain the glory* of our Lord Jesus Christ" (2 Thess. 2:13-14). We not only get salvation; we get God; we get glory – the Lord's glory in us and shining through us. Though by nature we "are lacking the glory of God" (Rom. 3:23 AT), He has provided the remedy in His Son, who is His Glory.

This process has already begun: "But we all, with face having been unveiled, beholding the glory of the Lord, we are being transformed into the same image from glory unto glory, as from the Lord, the Spirit" (2 Cor. 3:18, AT). Sinclair Ferguson helps us with his bluntness: "The startling significance of this might be plainer if we expressed it thus: the Spirit is given to glorify us...."[36] The Spirit takes from what is Christ's, His glory, and makes it known to us (Jn. 16:14). He enables us to behold

---

36. *The Holy Spirit*, 249, qtd. in Christopher W. Morgan, "Toward a Theology of the Glory of God," in *The Glory of God*, 185.

that glory. As we continue gazing at the beauty of Christ (cf. Ps. 27:4), the Spirit is changing us into His image with ever-increasing glory.[37] This astounding process will be completed at the second coming of Christ.

Jesus promised to return in "power and great glory."[38] His glory will be revealed, and all flesh will see it (1 Pet. 4:13, Isa. 40:5). We are "waiting for the happy hope and epiphany of the glory of our great God and Savior, Jesus Christ…" (Ti. 2:13, AT). Jesus is returning in His glory and in the glory of the Father, but also "to be *glorified in His saints"* (2 Thess. 1:10). When He is glorified in us, *we* will be glorified in Him (1:12).

Right now Christ "is filling *for Himself* all things in all ways," (Eph. 1:23, AT). In this series on the preeminence of Christ, let us be impacted fully by the revelation that the universe will be filled with *the glory of God* by being filled with *the life of Christ*, who *is* the Glory of God. So, we are now being filled and, at His coming, we will attain the fullness of Christ (4:13). When we see Him as He is, then our lowly bodies will be "raised in glory" and changed into spiritual, *glorified* bodies like His.[39] The glory of God in Christ will fill us entirely. Can you imagine how that will feel? Can you meditate on the greatest spiritual, emotional, and physical joys that we can experience in these bodies, and then imagine the joy of perfection[40] – sinlessly saturated with the glory, goodness, and gladness of the Spirit of God? This is our happy hope: *seeing and sharing in the glory of God* (Ti. 2:13, 1 Pet. 5:1). Is it not now crystal clear how God seeking His greatest glory in us is, in fact, the greatest good for us?

Immediately before Christ's epiphany, all of the natural stars will fall, and the world will go dark (Mt. 24:29, Rev. 6:12-17).

---

37. See the author's "Farewell Sermon: Behold the Glory of the Lord Jesus," 18 Aug 2013 (ProjectOne28.com/farewell). "With ever-increasing glory" is NIV's paraphrase of "from glory unto glory."

38. Mt. 16:27, 24:30, 25:31; Mk. 8:38, 13:26; Lk. 9:26, 21:27

39. Phil. 3:21; 1 Jn. 3:2-3; 1 Cor. 15:42-57, esp. v. 43 ("raised in glory")

Then Christ, the Light of the world, will shine in the east (Mt. 24:27, 30), and we will rise to meet Him, shining ourselves like stars because of His glory perfectly manifesting through our glorified bodies (Dan. 12:3, Mt. 13:43). As Isaiah 60:1-3 prophesied:

> Arise, shine, for your light has come,
>   and the glory of Yahweh has risen *upon you*.
> [2]For behold, darkness shall cover the earth,
>   and thick darkness the peoples;
> but Yahweh will arise *upon you*,
>   and his glory will be seen *upon you*.
> [3]And nations shall come to *your light*,
>   and kings to the brightness of *your rising*.

"When Christ who is your life appears, then you also will appear with him *in glory*" (Col. 3:4). Not only Christ will appear in glory, but because of Him, *we* will appear *in glory!* Then the world who hated us will know that King Jesus has loved us (Rev. 3:9). We have not suddenly become man-centered, because if the glory in us is Christ's glory, then Christ will get the glory for our glory. Romans 8:29, quoted above, gives the goal of our conformity to the image of God's Son, Jesus: "*for* Him to be the *firstborn* among many brothers." The ultimate purpose of our glorification is for Jesus to be seen to be the supreme heir, the preeminent One-of-a-kind Son.[41]

So far, we have applied only the first part of our definition for *glory:* we will receive and become the radiance of God's Being. The second part of the definition, I say blushingly, can be applied to us, as well: we will warrant praise and fame. C.

---

40. 1 Cor. 13:10-12: "the perfect comes" when we see Him "face to face."

41. That the Son is "the firstborn" (cf. Col. 1:15) does not mean that He was the first creature made, because He is fully God, eternally co-existent with the Father, and not made (see *Part Two*, 117-120). In the ancient world, "firstborn" could be used symbolically rather than literally, playing off the doubled inheritance (Dt. 21:17) and leadership exercised among his siblings. For example, David was the eighth and youngest son of Jesse, but God said, *"I will make him* the firstborn, *the highest* of the kings of the earth"* (Ps. 89:27). I.e., I will make him the supreme heir and leader of all. Such

S. Lewis beautifully related the disciple's requirement for child-like faith to the innocence and goodness in children's desire to be praised.[42] He is right. How often do we hear, "Daddy, see this! See this! Did you see me?" And I love to praise children – not only because it reenforces positive behavior, but because it gives them joy. Their faces light up. Their striving settles into satisfaction. Deep in the core of image-bearers burns a longing to be praised by God the Father.

My sin-mixed soul has often imagined compliments in the mouths of those reacting to my work. This surely exposes my pride's need to be fed, but I believe it is only a misdirection of the child-like need God has placed in me. As with many other sins, the problem is not the desire, but where we seek to satisfy it. Seeking glory from Man inhibits faith, but we *are* supposed to seek the glory that comes from God (Jn. 5:44). Sometimes when others are not sufficiently feeding our pride, we feed it ourselves (and encourage them to join in) by boasting. But, "the one commending himself, that one is not approved, but whom *the Lord commends*" (2 Cor. 10:18, AT). The second coming of Christ the Judge will expose every act and the purposes of every heart, "and then the *praise* will come ,to, each ,one, from God" (1 Cor. 4:5, AT). I would not dare say it, if it was not so clear in Scripture: God will commend and praise us!

Peter assured the chosen exiles that they were being guarded by God's power for full, final salvation (1 Pet. 1:4-5). Then:

> [6]In this you rejoice, though now for a little while, if necessary, you have been grieved by various trials, [7]so that the tested genuineness of your faith – more precious than gold that perishes though it is tested by fire – may be found to result in praise and glory and honor at the revelation of Jesus Christ.

preeminence is the point of Romans 8:29 (and Col. 1:15, cf. 1:18). Cf. Douglas J. Moo, *The Letters to the Colossians and to Philemon,* PNTC (Grand Rapids, MI: Eerdmans, 2008), 119-120.

42. "The Weight of Glory," in *The Weight of Glory: And Other Addresses* (New York:

The difficult interpretive question is whether this praise, glory, and honor will belong to Christ or to believers. Of course, Christ will receive it preeminently, but the context seems to favor believers as the recipients here.[43] Therefore, this beloved passage indeed confirms what we have seen in so many Scriptures above: we will receive praise, glory, and honor at the revelation of Christ, unto the praise, glory, and honor of its source, Christ Himself.

I imagine Jesus fulfilling His promise to confess my name before the Father: "Abba,[44] You remember Spencer; I was interceding for him earlier. He believed and confessed My Name. He worshiped in spirit and truth, and he spent himself seeking true worshipers for Us. Abba, I'm so excited to honor him in Our kingdom! Let's place him over five cities!" Then I imagine the response which Jesus motivated us to seek from the Master: "Well done, good and faithful servant!" (Mt. 25:21, 23). May it be so! When the God of the universe praises us, it will be a small thing in comparison that the nations will also praise us when they see our glory.[45]

The returning King will be praised for rewarding His saints and destroying the destroyers of the earth when He throws the false prophet, Antichrist, and his armies into the Lake of Fire and binds Satan in the abyss (Rev. 11:15-18, 19:1-7, 20-21). We will reign with Christ on earth for one thousand years (20:4-

---

HarperOne, 2001), 36-39. Child-like: Mk. 10:14-16, Lk. 18:16-17.

43. So also Alford, Henry, and Piper. The main theme of the section is the exiles' living hope, inheritance, and final salvation (vv. 3, 4, 5) contrasted with temporary tribulations. In the metaphor, the refined and proven gold is what is praised, glorified, and honored (v. 7). That gold is likened to (and surpassed by) faith, so it stands to reason that God will praise, glorify, and honor us because of the substance of our persevering faith. The paragraph closes with the same focus: believers receiving the end or goal of our faith, salvation (v. 9), which includes our glory. And finally, in the *inclusio* (like a bookend) of this very letter, Peter wrote: "And the God ,of, all grace, the ,One who, called you into His everlasting glory in Christ, ,after you have, suffered ,a, little, He Himself will restore, make firm, strengthen, ,and, establish ,you," (4:10, AT). Cf. also Rom. 2:7, 10.

44. The promise is in Mt. 10:32, Lk. 12:8, Rev. 3:5. *Abba* is Aramaic for "father."

45. E.g., Zeph. 3:20, Deut. 26:19, Isa. 61:6, 9; 62:2, 7; Jer. 30:19.

6), rebuilding the ancient ruins[46] and *making His resting place glorious* (Isa. 11:10, 60:13). Creation is groaning for this even now (Rom. 8:22), to "be set free from its bondage to corruption and obtain the freedom *of the glory of the children of God"* (8:21).

After the thousand years, Satan will be released from the abyss one last time, and He will deceive the unredeemed of the nations, enticing them to war against a restored Jerusalem (Rev. 20:7-9, Ezek. 38:8, 16). Fire will fall from heaven to consume them, and Satan will be thrown into the Lake of Fire to be tormented into the ages of the ages (Rev. 20:9-10, Ezek. 38:22). God prophesied through Ezekiel about His motivation for this battle:

> In the latter days I will bring you against my land, that the nations may *know me*, when through you, O Gog [cf. Rev. 20:8], *I vindicate my holiness* before their eyes (38:16).

> So *I will show my greatness and my holiness and make myself known* in the eyes of many nations. Then they will *know that I am Yahweh* (38:23).

> And *my holy name I will make known* in the midst of my people Israel, and I will not let *my holy name* be profaned anymore. And the nations shall *know that I am Yahweh*, the Holy One in Israel (39:7).

> … on the day that *I show my glory*, declares the Lord Yahweh (39:13).

> And *I will set my glory among the nations*, and all the nations shall *see my judgment* that I have executed, and my hand that I have laid on them. [22]The house of Israel shall *know that I am Yahweh* their God, from that day forward (39:21-22).

Therefore, we see – from the first kingdom conflict to the last – God acts for the glory of His Name among the peoples.

---

46. Isa. 58:12, 61:2-4; Am. 9:14; Ezek. 38:8. The timing in the paragraph above (and the one following it) reflects a classic premillennial view, which the author presently holds.

At the final judgment (Rev. 20:11-15), we will be honored to share in pronouncing judgment along with God and the Lamb, as we sit on His throne with authority to judge.[47] At this second resurrection, the resurrection of the unrighteous,[48] every knee will "bow, in heaven and on earth and under the earth, and *every tongue confess that Jesus Christ is Lord, to the glory of God the Father.*"[49] The unrepentant sinners, belatedly confessing the truth before everlasting judgment, will be ashamed, but we will rejoice to boast in Christ.[50]

> REVELATION 5:13 (AT)
> And I heard every creature in heaven and on earth and under the earth and on the sea, and all that is in them, saying, "To the One sitting on the throne and to the Lamb be the blessing and the honor and the glory and the might into the ages of the ages!"

Then God the Father will come down to tabernacle forever on the new, heavenly earth (Rev. 21:1-3). Christ, having defeated all enemies and summed up all things under His Headship, will hand over the kingdom to God the Father, and the Father will be "all in all" (1 Cor. 15:24-28, Eph. 1:9-10). Now we see the full, God-centered story. Before Creation, nothing existed except God; God was all. In the new creation, God will be all *in all*. Things will exist, and we will be here, but God's glory will fill every ounce of every thing.

New Jerusalem (the future us, as the Lamb's wife) is described as *"having the glory of God*, its radiance like a most rare

---

47. Rev. 20:4, 3:21; 1 Cor. 6:2-3

48. The "first resurrection" will be only believers (Rev. 20:4-6). The second is for unbelievers, described in 20:11-15. (That is, of course, *if* historic premillennialism is correct!) I believe Jesus also implicitly alluded to two distinct resurrections when He repeated the word twice in John 5:28-29: "...those who have done good to the resurrection of life, and those who have done evil to the resurrection of judgment" (cf. Dan. 12:2).

49. Phil. 2:10-11. See *Part Two*, 130-131, for the significance of this passage regarding the Godhood of Jesus.

50. Isa. 45:22-25, Phil. 3:3

jewel, like a jasper, clear as crystal" (Rev. 21:11). "And the city has no need of sun or moon to shine on it, for *the glory of God* gives it light, and its lamp is the Lamb" (21:23).[51] And "over all the glory there will be a marriage chamber,"[52] because we will be perfectly, faithfully, and eternally united to our Bridegroom King, the conquering Lamb.[53] With Christ, we will inherit all glorified things from our Father.[54] We will reign with Christ forever as kings and priests to our God.[55] Of the increase of His government and peace there will be no end (Isa. 9:6-7). For the coming ages, God will increasingly show us "the surpassing wealth of His *grace* [which is His *glory*, Ex. 34:6] in kindness toward us in Christ Jesus" – "unto the praise of the glory of His grace" (Eph. 2:7 and 1:6, AT).

Then, finally, God will have what He has been seeking from the beginning: a glory-filled creation that is full of the knowledge of His glory (Isa. 11:9, Hab. 2:14) and full of true worshipers from every tribe and language and people and nation who share His joy in His Son (Jn. 4:23-24, Rev. 5:9-10, 7:9). Amen; come quickly, Lord Jesus![56]

---

51. Cf. Isa. 60:19-20, Zech. 2:5.

52. Isa. 4:5 (AT). The word translated "canopy" (ESV, NASB, NIV) is used elsewhere only of the marriage chamber of a bridegroom and bride (Ps. 19:5, Joel 2:16; Motyer, *Isaiah*, 66). The word is related to a verb for covering, sheltering, shielding (Wolf, "*ḥāpap*," *TWOT*, 310). When married to the all-victorious King, in the Father's new world, we will be completely secure in Him.

53. Isa. 61:10, 62:5, Hos. 2:16-20, Mt. 9:15, 22:2, 25:1-13, Jn. 3:29, Rev. 19:7, 21:2, 9; 2 Cor. 11:2, Eph. 5:31-32

54. Rev. 21:7, 1 Cor. 3:21-23, Lk. 15:31

55. Rev. 1:6, 5:10, 20:6; cf. 1 Pet. 2:9-10 – in fulfillment of Ex. 19:5-6 (see p. 24).

56. Rev. 22:20

GOD'S GLORY, OUR JOY

The devil loves to lie to us that denying ourselves and living for God's glory will not be fun – that it means swearing off pleasure, being prudish, solemn, and dreadfully somber. Regrettably, many unhappy Christians reinforce the lie with their joyless lives. I zealously desire to destroy this stronghold at the close of this book.[1]

The truth is that God is the most joyous Being in existence. Scripture calls Him "the happy God."[2] Why is God eternally happy? The Father delights in the glory of the Son and Spirit, the Son in the Father and Spirit, the Spirit in the Father and Son.[3] This blissful Triune God created all things – including Man in His image – out of the overflow of His joy in His glory and in order to share His joy in His glory.[4]

---

1. For more, see the audio and expanded notes for "Delight in the Lord, Who Is Our Exceeding Joy" (ProjectOne28.com/joy) and especially the ministry of John Piper, e.g., the resources in n. 4 on p. 64.

2. Modern versions typically translate verses like 1 Tim. 1:11 and 6:15 as "the *blessed* God." However, Hebrew and Greek have two different word groups for "blessed" (spoken well of, Hb. *bārak*, Gk. *eulogeō*, not here) and "happy" (Hb. *'āshār*, Gk.

Therefore, we were made to be filled with the glory of the God of joy, to experience *in Him* the joy that surpasses anything this fallen world has to offer. God commands, "Delight yourself *in Yahweh*, and he will give you the desires of your heart" (Ps. 37:4). "Be rejoicing *in the Lord* always! Again I will say: be rejoicing!" (Phil. 4:4, AT). The psalmist sang, "You have put more joy in my heart than they have when their grain and their wine abound" (Ps. 4:7). He called God "my exceeding joy" or, literally, "the joy of my rejoicing" (43:4).[5] David sang, "You cause me to know the path of life; with Your face there is fullness of joys; at Your right hand, pleasures forevermore" (16:11, AT). There is the location of the greatest amount of joy possible for the longest amount of time possible: the face of Yahweh. Behold Him!

Jesus is our model of a joyful Man. He humbled Himself to take the form of a human Servant because *He delighted to do the Father's will* (Ps. 40:6-8, cf. Heb. 10:5-7). Perfectly aligned with the heart of His holy Father, He was anointed with gladness beyond any man (Ps. 45:6-7, Heb. 1:8-9).[6] He sold all that He had and "*endured the Cross for the joy* set before Him": returning to the Father's presence where there is fullness of joy and pleasures forevermore, as well as gaining a treasured Bride as His partner in advancing the kingdom of God on earth as in heaven.[7] Now, resurrected, He is in heaven, basking in the Triune joy. This joyful Christ lives in His disciples by His Spirit. He promised His resurrection would give His disciples joy that no one can take away (Jn. 16:22).

---

makarios, here). We should translate appropriately and celebrate this wonderful reality of God's glory. Cf., e.g., *TWOT*, 80; *NIDNTT*, 2:215-217; Grudem, *Systematic Theology*, 218-219; John Piper, *The Pleasures of God: Meditations on God's Delight in Being God* (Colorado Springs: Multnomah, 2012).

3. Prov. 8:30-31 (cf. 1 Cor. 1:24, 30; Col. 2:3), Isa. 42:1, Mt. 3:17, 17:5; Isa. 11:3

4. Prov. 8:30-31; Ps. 135:6, 115:3; and Ps. 16:11, Jn. 15:11, Mt. 25:21, 23

5. I cannot remember which John Piper message first tipped me off to the literal Hebrew construction. Cf. YLT, LITV, as well as NET study note.

6. See *Part Two*, 81-82, 126, for this passage's significance regarding Christ's Godhood.

This gospel is "good news *of great joy* for all the people," an offer to delight ourselves in the richest of food, the Bread of Life, Jesus Christ.[8] We saw in Chapter One that the essense of sin is not wanting God, not delighting in Him, but instead taking greater pleasure in lesser things.[9] That kind of heart will never respond rightly to the gospel. Thanks be to God: He promises to give new hearts that love Him by His Spirit.[10] "Grace is God's giving us sovereign joy in God that triumphs over joy in sin."[11]

The call to discipleship is a call to come and die to the two-bit, temporary pleasures of this evil age in order to live in the joyous Christ, in God. In one of the most significant passages on the nature of discipleship,[12] Jesus stated that His teaching (and His disciples' obedience) was purposed to result in *His joy* becoming *their joy:*

> These things I have spoken to you, that my joy may be in you, and that your joy may be full (Jn. 15:11).

Can you fathom the thought of the infinite joy of God the Son *in* you? "…that your joy may be full" – what a modest description!

Therefore, the path to the fullest joy now and in eternity is being a disciple who abides in Christ and in His words, obeying and bearing fruit for God's glory. Our rebellious souls have twisted "obedience" into a negative word when, truly, obedience is supposed to be motivated by joy and rewarded with joy.[13] Because we strive for our own sovereignty, we misinterpret God's commands

---

7. Mt. 13:44, Heb. 12:2, Ps. 16:11. This sentence is unpacked in "Delight in the Lord, Our Exceeding Joy" (ProjectOne28.com/joy).

8. Lk. 2:10, Isa. 55:1-2, Jn. 6:35-58

9. See pp. 19-21.

10. E.g., Dt. 30:6, Ezek. 11:19-20, 36:25-27

11. John Piper, *The Legacy of Sovereign Joy: God's Triumphant Grace in the Lives of Augustine, Luther, and Calvin* (Wheaton, IL: Crossway, 2000), 57 (emphasis removed).

12. Jn. 15; see p. 73.

13. Ps. 40:8, Mt. 25:21, 23. We *must* serve/obey *joyfully* (Deut. 28:47–48, Ps. 100:2).

as limiting our supposedly paramount freedom. "Thou shalt not commit adultery," for example, can seem as though God is withholding rightful pleasures in other women. But God is a good Father. If He withholds, it is to free you to receive something better – an untainted, faithful, spiritual marriage to one godly woman who will be your delight.[14] Adultery bears rotten fruit; God's commands, even His prohibitions, are "for your good" (Deut. 10:13). When we offer our bodies as living sacrifices, then we "*approve*" God's will to be "good, *pleasing*, and perfect" (Rom. 12:1-2 NIV). When we believe obediently, we please God and come to know His pleasure in communion with Him (Heb. 11:6). What could be better?

The problem with sin is not that we seek pleasure, but that we misdirect our desire to fleeting rip-offs instead of the eternal pleasures and fullness of joy in the presence of Yahweh (Ps. 16:11, 4:7). C. S. Lewis wrote:

> Indeed, if we consider the unblushing promises of reward and the staggering nature of the rewards promised in the Gospels, it would seem that our Lord finds our desires, not too strong, but too weak. We are half-hearted creatures, fooling about with drink and sex and ambition when infinite joy is offered us, like an ignorant child who wants to go on making mud pies in a slum because he cannot imagine what is meant by the offer of a holiday at the sea. We are far too easily pleased.[15]

Pray that the Spirit, when you face temptation, will remind you that the sinful offer is only a rip-off of what you really want: joy in the Lord and the good He gives to enjoy.[16] God bids us to drink from the river of His delights, His very Spirit![17]

---

14. Deut. 24:5, Prov. 5:18-19, SS 7:6 [Ezek. 24:16]. I still remembered this teaching and example from eleven years prior in the book or workbook for *Experiencing God: Knowing and Doing the Will of God* by Henry Blackaby and Claude V. King.

15. "The Weight of Glory," in *The Weight of Glory: And Other Addresses* (New York: HarperOne, 2001), 25, an essay which brought tears to my eyes and grew my heart.

16. 1 Tim. 6:17. This is why sinful passions are called "deceitful desires" (Eph. 4:22); they lie as though sin is what we really want. See "The Present Profitability of Piety" (ProjectOne28.com/piety) for more, e.g., the expulsive power of a superior pleasure.

At the core of idolatry is delight in some person or some thing as though it is more valuable and more delightful than God. At the core of worship is delight in the infinite worth of God.[18] Praise is the natural overflow of that joy. Lewis wrote:

> ...all enjoyment spontaneously overflows into praise unless (sometimes even if) shyness or the fear of boring others is deliberately brought in to check it. The world rings with praise – lovers praising their mistresses, readers their favourite poet, walkers praising the countryside, players praising their favorite game – praise of weather, wines, dishes, actors, motors, horses, colleges, countries, historical personages, children, flowers, mountains....

> ...just as men spontaneously praise whatever they value, so they spontaneously urge us to join them in praising it: "Isn't she lovely? Wasn't it glorious? Don't you think that magnificent?" The Psalmists in telling everyone to praise God are doing what all men do when they speak of what they care about....

> *I think we delight to praise what we enjoy because the praise not merely expresses but completes the enjoyment; it is its appointed consummation.* It is not out of compliment that lovers keep on telling one another how beautiful they are; the delight is incomplete till it is expressed. ...The worthier the object, the more intense this delight would be.[19]

God is infinitely worthy. Even dim glimpses of His beauty cause disciples to rejoice in Him with "glorified joy"[20] that overflows in praise and service. This is the glory God deserves. Jonathan Edwards wrote:

---

17. Ps. 36:7-9 fulfilled in Jn. 7:37-39 (cf. definition of idolatry in Jer. 2:12-13)

18. Consider how often the God-breathed worship book, the Psalms, *commands* us to rejoice, exult, delight, and be glad in the Lord (e.g., 5:11, 14:7, 32:11, 33:1, 40:16, 47:1, 48:11, 53:6, 64:10, 66:1, 67:4, 68:4, 81:1, 95:1-2, 97:12, 98:4, 100:1-2, 105:3, 118:24, 132:9, 149:2, 149:5).

19. "A Word About Praising," in *Reflections on the Psalms* (San Diego: Harcourt, 1986), 94-96 (emphasis mine).

20. 1 Pet. 1:8 (AT)

> [The] glory of God [does not] consist in merely the creature's
> perceiving his perfections; for the creature may perceive the
> power and wisdom of God, and yet take no delight in it, but
> abhor it.[21] Those creatures that so do, don't glorify God....
> This glory of God, therefore, [consists] in the creature's
> admiring and rejoicing [and] exulting[22] in the manifestation
> of his beauty and excellency.... The essence of glorifying...
> God consists, therefore, in the creature's rejoicing in God's
> manifestations of his beauty....[23]

Do you delight in the beauty and excellency of God? Does
the revelation of His glory move you to live for His fame? Is
every aspect of your life affected by and aimed at the glory of His
Name? Will you seek the glory of His Name at any cost? These
are no light questions, but ones worth pondering, while looking
at yourself in the mirror and praying (e.g., Ps. 86:4, 85:6, 90:14).

A Final Appeal

C. S. Lewis noticed "the humblest, and at the same time
most balanced and capacious, minds praised most, while the
cranks, misfits, and malcontents praised least... praise almost
seems to be inner health made audible."[24] I have written this book
to demonstrate God's passion for His glory in the preeminence
of Christ and to show that *the foundation and all-encompassing
passion of a disciple's life must be God's glory in the preeminence of
Christ.* Such passion, such jealousy, I believe, is the difference
between the healthy and the unhealthy, the happy and the
unhappy, the sane and the depraved, the loving and the hating,
the hot and the lukewarm, the obedient and the rebellious, the
enduring and the stumbling – the difference between disciples
and broken off branches.[25]

---

21. Satan and the demons believe without delight (see Jas. 2:19 and p. 75).

22. To exult is to boast, to rejoice triumphantly, feeling and showing jubilation.

23. "Nothing Upon Earth Can Represent the Glories of Heaven," in *The Works of
Jonathan Edwards*, Vol. 14, ed. Kenneth P. Minkema (New Haven, CT: Yale
University Press, 1997), 144, as qtd. in John Piper, *Don't Waste Your Life*, 30.

24. *Reflections on the Psalms*, 94.

Dear reader, I make my appeal once more: God is worthy! Infinitely more excellent than all! Be broken-hearted for so often preferring lesser things above your Creator and Redeemer. Repent. Today and every day, fix your eyes on Christ, the radiance of God's glory, and pray for a spirit of wisdom and revelation to see Him more clearly.[26] As we are gazing at His beauty, beholding His glory, His Spirit will be transforming us into His image from glory to glory.[27] We will find it a sheer joy – the only worthwhile and enduring joy – to live wholly for Him.

> And ˌtoˌ the ˌOneˌ being powerful to keep you free from stumbling and ˌtoˌ cause youˌ to stand *before His glory blameless with jubilation* – [25]ˌtoˌ the only God our Savior through Jesus Christ our Lord ˌbeˌ *glory*, majesty, might, and authority before every age and now and into all the ages; amen![28]

---

25. For "broken off branches," in such a sentence, see Jn. 15:1-11, esp. vv. 2, 6, 8, 11.

26. Heb. 12:2, 1:3; Eph. 1:17-18

27. Ps. 27:4, 2 Cor. 3:18

28. Jude 24-25 (AT). See *Part Two*, 139, for this significance of this passage regarding the Godhood of Christ.

APOSTOLIC DOXOLOGIES

Doxology is built from the Greek *doxa* ("glory") and *logos* ("word"). Hence, a doxology is a word of glory, ascribing glory that is due. I did not work most of the apostles' doxologies into the body of this book because they really belong in a category of their own. Just in case anyone glosses over them when reading Scripture, as though such verses are an aside, I am listing them here with the proposal that these verses make crystal clear the apostles' priority in all things: the glory of God through Jesus Christ. May we imitate them as they imitated Christ.[1]

Rom. 1:25: "…the Creator, who is blessed into the ages; amen!"[2]

Rom. 9:5: "…the Christ, the One, being God over all, blessed into the ages; amen!"[3]

Rom. 11:33-36: "Oh, the depth of the wealth and wisdom and

---

1.   1 Cor. 4:16, 11:1; Phil. 3:17; 1 Thess. 1:6; 2 Thess. 3:9

2.   All of these doxologies come from the author's translations.

3.   For its significance regarding the Godhood of Christ, See *Part Two*, 124-125.

knowledge ,of, God! How unsearchable ,are, His judgments and untraceable His ways! [34]'For who knew ,the, mind ,of the, Lord, or who became His counselor?' [35]'Or who gave to Him and will be repaid ,by, Him?' [36]Because from Him and through Him and unto Him ,are, all things – to Him ,be,[4] the glory into the ages; amen!"

Rom. 16:25-27: "And ,to, the ,One, being powerful to strengthen you according to my gospel and the proclamation ,of, Jesus Christ, according to ,the, revelation ,of the, secret having been kept silent ,for the, times ,of the, ages, [26]but now having been manifested also through ,the, prophetic writings according to ,the, command ,of, the eternal God, having been made known to all the peoples unto ,the, obedience ,of, faith – [27]to the, only wise God, through Jesus Christ, ,be, the glory into the ages; amen!"

Gal. 1:4-5: "…our God and Father, [5]to, whom ,be, the glory into the ages ,of, the ages; amen!"

Eph. 3:20-21: "And ,to, the ,One, being powerful to do exceedingly beyond all that we ask or imagine according to the power working in us, [21]to, Him ,be, the glory in the Assembly and in Christ Jesus unto all the generations ,of, the age ,of, the ages; amen!"

Phil. 4:19-20: "And my God will fill your every need, according to His wealth in glory in Christ Jesus. [20]And ,to, our God and

---

4. One of the most significant translation challenges, in my mind, is whether or not doxologies should be translated "blessed [be]" or "blessed [is]." The verb is not present in the original Greek, only implied. The question is whether or not an indicative or optative mood is implied. Is it a statement of fact, "God *is* blessed – by angels and by the Church now and forever"? Or is it a wish, a prayer, "*May* God *be* blessed by me and my readers now and forever"? The major translations opt for a prayer, while several respected exegetes lobby for a declaration. To be honest, I cannot make up my mind. The "be" translations in this appendix are mainly because I cannot yet accrue enough confidence in an "is" translation to depart from the judgment of the major translation committees. See Peter T. O'Brien, "Benediction, Blessing, Doxology, Thanksgiving," in *Dictionary of Paul and His Letters*, ed. Gerald F. Hawthorne and Ralph P. Martin (Downers Grove, IL: InterVarsity Press, 1993), 68–71. Cf. n. 5 below.

Father be the glory into the ages of the ages; amen!"

1 Tim. 1:17: "And to the King of the ages, immortal, unseen, the only God, be honor and glory into the ages of the ages; amen!"

1 Tim. 6:15-16: "… the happy and only Sovereign, the King of the ones kinging and Lord of the ones lording, [16]the only One having immorality, dwelling in unapproachable light, whom no one among men has seen, nor is being able to see – to whom be honor and eternal might; amen!"

2 Tim. 4:18: "…to whom be the glory into the ages of the ages; amen!"

Heb. 13:21: "…to whom be the glory into the ages; amen!"

1 Pet. 4:11: "…in order that in all things God may be being glorified through Jesus Christ, to whom is the glory and might into the ages of the ages; amen!"[5]

1 Pet. 5:11: "…to Him be the might into the ages; amen!"

2 Pet. 3:18: "…but be growing in the grace and knowledge of our Lord and Savior, Jesus Christ. To Him be the glory both now and into the day of eternity!"

Jude 1:24-25: "And to the One being powerful to keep you free from stumbling and to cause you to stand before His glory blameless with jubilation – [25]to the only God our Savior through Jesus Christ our Lord be glory, majesty, might, and authority before every age and now and into all the ages; amen!"[6]

---

5. Unlike the other doxologies (cf. n. 4), the verb is actually present here, and it is in the indicative form, "to whom *is* the glory." George W. Knight III argues that the presence of the verb here should convince us that all of the doxologies without the verb should also be translated like this (*The Pastoral Epistles*, NIGTC [Grand Rapids, MI: Eerdmans, 1992], 106). However, the opposite argument could be made: the verb is left out when implying the optative and only inserted when necessary to explicate a different meaning, the indicative. As I said in n. 4, I don't really know.

6. See *Part Two*, 139, for its significance regarding the Godhood of Christ.

Rev. 1:5-6: "…and from Jesus Christ, the faithful witness, the firstborn ,of, the dead, and the ruler ,of, the kings ,of, the earth. ,To, the ,One who, is loving us and released us from our sins by His blood, ⁶and made us ,a, kingdom, priests ,to, His God and Father – ,to, Him ,be, the glory and the might into the ages ,of, the ages; amen!"

Yes and amen!

ACKNOWLEDGMENTS

As I contemplated acknowledgments for this book on the glory of God, I was overwhelmed with a sense of how many people God used to show me His glory and grow my passion for Him. It really is a beautiful work our Lord is doing, in the midst of our weaknesses, as He builds and sanctifies His bride.

I'm grateful to God that my parents raised me at First Baptist Church in El Dorado, KS. But I had only minimal, external religious rituals; Nathan Hiebert had Jesus. When I became a freshman on the varsity basketball team, I buddied up with this sophomore teammate, bumming rides to practices and hoping the upperclassmen wouldn't beat us up. But the providence of God was bigger than that. The integrity of Nathan's walk and the faithfulness of his words showed me the matchless worth of Jesus, and, suddenly, I found Jesus, as He is clothed in the Gospel, to be compellingly beautiful. Like a big brother, Nathan continued to be the biggest influence in my spiritual walk through high school and into college. Years after being the Best Man in each other's weddings, we still get together, and his faithful leadership of his family and his church still encourage me.

In my first couple of years as a disciple, FBC didn't have a senior pastor or a youth pastor. I thank God for the adults who spent themselves on us youth and blew on the baby fire in my heart, saints such as Hal and Rita Neukirch, Randy and Chris Crank, Jim Zang, Cathy Cuckler, Martha Sturgill, and Todd Kurimsky. I'm also grateful for Steve Appleman and the praise team in those days for enabling me to express what was happening in my heart. Just the other day (about twenty years later), I woke up to my heart singing, "Shine, Jesus, Shine" (and pictured Chris Crank smiling up at me in the balcony).

Then the Lord brought us a senior pastor in Wade Graber, who inspired my faith. In the same year, the Lord brought a youth pastor, Mike Chappell and his wife Kim, who both skillfully helped to mature me and my soon-to-be bride. The Lord was at work in those days, and friends fanned the flame in my heart, such as Scott and Janice (Bechtold) Appleman, Josh Adams, Garrett Klassen, Anthony Carver, Danial Porter, Roger Briggs, Angela (Royse) Murphy, and Toad.

Through Pastor Mike, the Lord connected me with Chris Waipa just when I was asking big questions about ministry and my calling. Chris came preaching a fiery message of repentant worship for the sake of the glory of the holy God. It struck a chord in my heart that I wanted to keep playing. Through serving his ministry, I continued to grow in zeal and understanding, and the outline for this book first began to take shape in those days.

I thank God also for my next mentor, Sam McVay, Jr., who passionately spurred us to be "obsessive-compulsive" about Christ and acted as a spiritual father in the most formative period of my spiritual life. Many of my foundational convictions came from his teachings, but more than the content, I benefitted most from the times I acted fleshly, and he chastened me as a father would a son.

The people at New Life created a wonderful context to grow up and grow in our gifts. Doc and Tamsel Kuhns blessed us in many ways, especially in a family-like house church. Brock McKay encouraged unlike any other. Throughout an entire decade of ministry at New Life, Jonathan Brickley was my closest brother and accountability partner; I'm eternally grateful because I can imagine where I'd be without him. Other brothers also gave strength and joy, such as Chris Gifford, Al Wilkinson, Caleb McNary, Ryan Vandenberg, Levi Keplar, Scott Starr, Mark Habluetzel, Toby Kriwiel, and Shem Hatfield. Tyler Norris, who labored diligently and graciously with his impressive skills to design this book's cover and to help me develop ProjectOne28.com, has been as good of a friend as anyone could want, always stirring me to believe and obey.

I am especially thankful to my colleague at Veritas, Mrs. Jonnie Finger, for her graciousness in editing and improving this work. Any enduring errors or weaknesses, of course, belong not to her, but to me.

I adore God's glory in no other person on earth more fully than in my wife, Amber. She is more than I even knew to hope for. Her beauty, mercy, and felicity are rivaled only by the glorious children she has borne and is raising with such grace. I behold them and know that there is a God who is manifesting His glory through His creations.

To the Father of every good gift be all glory now and into the ages!

SELECT BIBLIOGRAPHY

Athanasius, *De Synodis* 51 (ccel.org/ccel/schaff/npnf204.xxii.ii.iii.html).

Aalen, Sverre, "Glory, Honour," *New International Dictionary of New Testament Theology*, Vol. 2, ed. Colin Brown (Grand Rapids, MI: Zondervan, 1986), 44-52.

Bauer, William, *A Greek-English Lexicon of the New Testament and Other Early Christian Literature,* Third Edition, Rev. and ed. Frederick William Danker (Chicago and London: The University of Chicago Press, 2000).

Beale, G. K., *A New Testament Biblical Theology: The Unfolding of the Old Testament in the New* (Grand Rapids, MI: Baker Academic, 2011).

—— *The Temple and the Church's Mission: A Biblical Theology of the Dwelling Place of God*, ed. D. A. Carson (Downers Grove, IL: InterVarsity Press, 2004).

Beitenhard, Hans, "Name," *New International Dictionary of New Testament Theology*, Vol. 2, ed. Colin Brown (Grand Rapids, MI: Zondervan, 1986), 648-656.

Brown, Colin, "Head," *New International Dictionary of New Testament Theology*, Vol. 2, ed. Colin Brown (Grand Rapids, MI: Zondervan, 1986), 156-163.

Carson, D. A., *Exegetical Fallacies*, Second Edition (Grand Rapids, MI: Baker Academic, 1996).

—— *The Gospel according to John,* The Pillar New Testament Commentary, ed. D. A. Carson (Grand Rapids, MI: Eerdmans, 1991).

—— "What Is the Gospel? Revisited," in *For the Fame of God's Name: Essays in Honor of John Piper*, ed. Sam Storms and Justin Taylor (Wheaton, IL: Crossway, 2010).

Chesterton, G. K., "Introduction to the Book of Job" (chesterton.org/introduction-to-job).

Coppes, Leonard J., "*qānā*," *Theological Wordbook of the Old Testament,* ed. R. Laird Harris, Gleason L. Archer, Jr., and Bruce K. Waltke (Chicago, IL: Moody Publishers, 1980), 802-803.

Durham, John, *Exodus*, Word Biblical Commentary (Nashville: Thomas Nelson, 1987).

Edwards, Jonathan, "Nothing Upon Earth Can Represent the Glories of Heaven," in *The Works of Jonathan Edwards*, Vol. 14, ed. Kenneth P. Minkema (New Haven, CT: Yale University Press, 1997).

Geisler, Norman L., *A Popular Survey of the Old Testament* (Grand Rapids, MI: BakerBooks, 2007).

Gentry, Peter J., "Kingdom through Covenant: Humanity as the Divine Image," *SBJT* 12/1 [2008]: 16-42.

Gentry, Peter J., and Stephen J. Wellum, *God's Kingdom through God's Covenants: A Concise Biblical Theology* (Wheaton, IL: Crossway, 2015).

Goetzmann, Jürgen, "House, Build, Manage, Steward," in *New International Dictionary of New Testament Theology*, Vol. 2, ed. Colin Brown (Grand Rapids, MI: Zondervan, 1986), 247-256.

Grudem, Wayne, *Systematic Theology: An Introduction to Biblical Doctrine* (Grand Rapids, MI: Zondervan, 2000).

Hamilton, James M., Jr., *God's Glory in Salvation through Judgment: A Biblical Theology* (Wheaton, IL: Crossway, 2010).

—— "The Skull Crushing Seed of the Woman: Inner-Biblical Interpretation of Genesis 3:15," *SBJT* 10:2 (Summer 2006), 30-54 (free at jimhamilton.info/wp-content/uploads/2008/04/hamilton_sbjt_10-2.pdf).

Hamilton, Victor, P., "*shadday*," *Theological Wordbook of the Old Testament*, ed. R. Laird Harris, Gleason L. Archer, Jr., and Bruce K. Waltke (Chicago, IL: Moody Publishers, 1980), 907.

Jones, Floyd Nolen, *The Chronology of the Old Testament*, 16th Edition (Green Forest, AR: MasterBooks, 1993-2004).

Knight, George W., III, *The Pastoral Epistles*, The New International Greek Testament Commentary (Grand Rapids, MI: Eerdmans, 1992).

Köstenberger, Andreas J., *John*, Baker Exegetical Commentary on the New Testament (Grand Rapids, MI: Baker Academic, 2004).

Köstenberger, Andreas J., and Scott R. Swain, *Father, Son, and Spirit: The Trinity and John's Gospel* (Downers Grove, IL: IVP Academic, 2008).

Ladd, George Eldon, *A Theology of the New Testament*, Revised Edition, ed. Donald A. Hagner (Grand Rapids: Eerdmans, 1993).

Lewis, C. S., "A Word About Praising," in *Reflections on the Psalms* (San Diego: Harcourt, 1986).

—— "The Weight of Glory," in *The Weight of Glory: And Other Addresses* (New York: HarperOne, 2001).

Longman III, Tremper, "The Glory of God in the Old Testament," in *The Glory of God*, Theology in Community, ed. Christopher W. Morgan & Robert A. Peterson (Wheaton, IL: Crossway, 2010).

McConville, J. G., "Ezra-Nehemiah and the Fulfillment of Prophecy," *Vetus Testamentum*, Vol. 36, Fasc. 2 (Apr., 1986), 205-224.

McVay, Jr., Sam, "1 Chronicles 15," 6 Feb 2011 (NewLifeEquip.com/resourcelibrary.cfm?id=8964).

—— "The Supremacy of Christ," 12 Sept 2004 (NewLifeEquip.com/resourcelibrary.cfm?id=8592).

McVay, Jr., Sam, and Spencer Stewart, *Introduction to Disciple-making: Obeying the Global Mandate of the Resurrected King Jesus* (El Dorado, KS: Project one28, 2013).

—— *The Model Prayer: Jesus Said, "Be Praying in This Manner"* (El Dorado, KS: Project one28, 2013).

—— *Spirit, Soul, Body: The Blueprint of Man in the Image of God* (El Dorado, KS: Project one28, 2010).

Melick, Jr., Richard R., "The Glory of God in the Synoptic Gospels, Acts, and the General Epistles," in *The Glory of God*, Theology in Community, ed. Christopher W. Morgan & Robert A. Peterson (Wheaton, IL: Crossway, 2010).

Moo, Douglas J., *The Epistle to the Romans,* New International Commentary on the New Testament (Grand Rapids, MI: Eerdmans, 1996).

—— *The Letters to the Colossians and to Philemon,* Pillar New Testament

Commentary, ed. D. A. Carson (Grand Rapids, MI: Eerdmans, 2008).

Morgan, Christopher W., "Toward a Theology of the Glory of God," in *The Glory of God*, Theology in Community, ed. Christopher W. Morgan & Robert A. Peterson (Wheaton, IL: Crossway, 2010).

Motyer, J. Alec, *The Prophecy of Isaiah: An Introduction & Commentary* (Downers Grove, IL: IVP Academic, 1993).

—— "The Revelation of the Divine Name" (Tyndale Press, 1959), now free at TheologicalStudies.org.uk/article_revelation_motyer.html.

Murray, Andrew, *Humility: The Beauty of Holiness* (New York: Anson D. F. Randolph & Co., free at manybooks.net/titles/murrayaother08Humility. html).

O'Brien, Peter T., "Benediction, Blessing, Doxology, Thanksgiving," in *Dictionary of Paul and His Letters*, ed. Gerald F. Hawthorne and Ralph P. Martin (Downers Grove, IL: InterVarsity Press, 1993).

—— *The Letter to the Ephesians,* The Pillar New Testament Commentary, ed. D. A. Carson (Grand Rapids, MI: Eerdmans, 1999).

Osborne, Grant R., *Revelation,* Baker Exegetical Commentary on the New Testament (Grand Rapids, MI: Baker Academic, 2002).

Oswalt, John N., "*bārak,*" *Theological Wordbook of the Old Testament,* ed. R. Laird Harris, Gleason L. Archer, Jr., and Bruce K. Waltke (Chicago, IL: Moody Publishers, 1980), 132.

Piper, John, "Christian Hedonism: Forgive the Label, But Don't Miss the Truth," 1 Jan 1995 (desiringGod.org/articles/christian-hedonism).

—— "Christian Hedonism with Questions and Answers," 1 Jan 1998 (desiringGod.org/messages/christian-hedonism-with-questions-and-answers).

—— *Desiring God: Meditations of a Christian Hedonist* (Sisters, OR: Multnomah, 2003).

—— *Don't Waste Your Life* (Wheaton, IL: Crossway Books, 2003).

—— "God Is Most Glorified in Us When We Are Most Satisfied in Him," 13 Oct 2012 (desiringGod.org/messages/god-is-most-glorified-in-us-when-we-are-most-satisfied-in-him).

—— *God Is the Gospel: Meditations on God's Love as the Gift of Himself* (Wheaton, IL: Crossway, 2005).

—— *God's Passion for His Glory: Living the Vision of Jonathan Edwards* (Wheaton, IL: Crossway, 1998).

—— "The Image of God: An Approach from Biblical and Systematic Theology." *Studia Biblica et Theologica* 1:1 (March 1971), available at desiringGod.org/articles/the-image-of-god.

—— "Let the Peoples Praise You, O God, Let All the Peoples Praise You!" 20 Sept 2011 (desiringGod.org/messages/let-the-peoples-praise-you-o-god-let-all-the-peoples-praise-you).

—— *Let the Nations Be Glad: The Supremacy of God in Missions*, Third Edition (Grand Rapids, MI: Baker Academic, 2010).

—— "Rebuilding Some Basics of Bethlehem: The Centrality of the Glory of God," 4 Nov 2009 (desiringGod.org/articles/rebuilding-some-basics-of-bethlehem-the-centrality-of-the-glory-of-god).

—— "Sin Prefers Anything to God," Ask Pastor John, Episode 570, 8 Apr 2015 (desiringGod.org/interviews/sin-prefers-anything-to-god).

—— *Spectacular Sins: And Their Global Purpose in the Glory of Christ* (Wheaton, IL: Crossway, 2008).

—— *The Dangerous Duty of Delight: Daring to Make God Your Greatest Treasure* (Colorado Springs: Multnomah, 2011).

—— "The Glory of God in the Sight of Eternity," 26 July 2013 (desiringGod.org/messages/do-not-lose-heart).

—— *The Legacy of Sovereign Joy: God's Triumphant Grace in the Lives of Augustine, Luther, and Calvin* (Wheaton, IL: Crossway, 2000).

—— *The Pleasures of God: Meditations on God's Delight in Being God* (Colorado Springs: Multnomah, 2012).

—— "To Him Be Glory Forevermore," 17 Dec 2006 (desiringGod.org/messages/to-him-be-glory-forevermore).

—— "Treasuring Christ and the Call to Suffer: Part 2," 6 Sept 2007 (desiringGod.org/messages/treasuring-christ-and-the-call-to-suffer-part-2).

—— "What Does It Mean to Be Made in God's Image?" Ask Pastor John, Episode 153, 19 Aug 2013 (desiringGod.org/interviews/what-does-it-mean-to-be-made-in-god-s-image).

—— "What is God's glory?" 6 Jul 2009 (desiringGod.org/interviews/what-is-gods-glory).

—— "What Is Sin? The Essence and Root of All Sinning," 2 Feb 2015 (desiringGod.org/messages/the-origin-essence-and-definition-of-sin).

—— "Why Oprah and Brad Pitt Deserted God (And Why You Shouldn't)" (vimeo.com/51407893).

Reeves, Michael, *Delighting in the Trinity: An Introduction to the Christian Faith* (Downers Grove, IL: InterVarsity Press, 2012).

Reidhead, Paris, "Then Shekels and a Shirt,"(ParisReidheadBibleTeaching Ministries.org/Ten_Shekels_and_A_Shirt.html and SermonIndex.net/modules/mydownloads/singlefile.php?lid=282).

Rengstorf, Karl Heinrich, "Jesus Christ, Nazarene, Christian," *New International Dictionary of New Testament Theology*, Vol. 2, ed. Colin Brown (Grand Rapids, MI: Zondervan, 1986), 330-348.

Ross, Allen P., *A Commentary on the Psalms*, Vol. 1 (1-41), Kegel Exegetical Library (Grand Rapids, MI: Kregel, 2011).

Schreiner, Thomas R., "A Biblical Theology of the Glory of God," in *For the Fame of God's Name: Essays in Honor of John Piper*, ed. Sam Storms and Justin Taylor (Wheaton, IL: Crossway, 2010).

Stewart, Spencer, "A Celebration of Propitiation" (ProjectOne28.com/good-friday).

—— "Delight in the Lord, Who Is Our Exceeding Joy," 11 Dec 2011 (ProjectOne28.com/joy).

—— "Farewell Sermon: Behold the Glory of the Lord Jesus," 18 Aug 2013 (ProjectOne28.com/farewell).

—— "HIStory: Session 7, The Exile and the Prophetic Promises" (ProjectOne28.com/HIStory).

—— "Introduction to the Old Testament" (ProjectOne28.com/ OTsurvey).

—— *Light Shines in the Darkness: Scripture Interpreting the Spiritual Drama of Genesis 1:2-3* (El Dorado, KS: Project one28, 2010).

—— "Loving God and Loving Each Other for the Glory of God," 10 Apr 2011 (ProjectOne28.com/loving-each-other).

—— "Psalm 8: What Is Man? A Worshiping Warrior" (ProjectOne28. com/psalm8).

—— "Righteousness and Justice: The Foundation of God's Throne," 16 Oct 2011 (ProjectOne28.com/justice).

—— "The Hardening of Pharaoh (and Millions of Others)" (ProjectOne28.com/hardening).

—— *The Preeminence of Christ: Part Two, The I AM* (Lawrence, KS: Project one28, 2017).

—— *Theology 101 for Kids!* (ProjectOne28.com/kids).

—— "Trusting God Is Good When Bad Happens," 26 Jun 2011 (ProjectOne28.com/Job).

—— "Tying the Two Testaments Together: Part Two" (ProjectOne28. com/testaments).

The NET Bible, Copyright © 1996-2005 Biblical Studies Press. Used by permission.

Weins, Gary, "The Father of Humility," *Come to Papa* (burningheartministries. com/Store/Products/1000011436/BHM_Store_products/MP3_ Downloads/Come_to_Papa.aspx).

Wolf, Herbert, *"ḥāpap," Theological Wordbook of the Old Testament*, ed. R. Laird Harris, Gleason L. Archer, Jr., and Bruce K. Waltke (Chicago, IL:

Moody Publishers, 1980), 310.

Wright, Christopher J. H., *Knowing God the Father Through the Old Testament* (Downers Grove, IL: IVP Academic, 2007).

—— "Who Are We and What Are We Here For? The Identity and Calling of God's People," AGTS Spring Lectureship, 21 Jan 2010 (http://www.agts.edu/news/news_archives/2010_1_19spring_lectureship.html).

SELECT SCRIPTURE INDEX

The Preeminence of Christ:
Part Two, The I AM

Introduction to Disciple-making:
Obeying the Global Mandate of the Resurrected King Jesus

The Basics:
The Beginning, the Gospel of God's Grace, and the New Beginning

The Kingdom of God:
The Reason Christ Created Man, Became Man, and Is Coming Again

Light Shines in the Darkness:
Scripture Interpreting the Spiritual Drama of Genesis 1:2-3

Spirit, Soul, Body:
The Blueprint of Man in the Image of God

Spiritual Gifts:
Discovering Graces and Partnering to Manifest the Fullness of Christ

The Model Prayer:
Jesus Said, "Be Praying In This Manner"

Why Trust the Bible?

Theology 101 for Kids!

Free at ProjectOne28.com